A Comprehensive Guide To United States Commemorative Coins

by
James S. Iacovo

The Ivy Press, Incorporated
Dallas, Texas

© 1979, James S. Iacovo
Library of Congress Catalogue Card #78-71956
ISBN # 0-933372-00-0

Printed in the United States of America. All rights reserved.
No reproduction in whole or in part permitted without
the express written consent of the author.

Published by
The Ivy Press, Incorporated
7515 Greenville Avenue, Suite 800
Dallas, Texas 75231

Preface

This book is dedicated to the many collectors around the country who believe, as this author does, that collecting U.S. silver and gold commemoratives for profit or pleasure is one of the most challenging and rewarding areas of numismatics.

If A Comprehensive Guide convinces a few more people to begin collecting commemorative coins and educates many others on the proper grading, scarcity, and investment potential of "commems", it will have served a useful purpose.

Acknowledgements

Many people were involved in the writing of this book the past two years. The contributions of the following were particularly significant:

My wife Linda, who at first was extremely skeptical of my efforts, but in the end gave her complete support.

My two daughters, Michelle and Lisa, who put up with their dad's absence on too many occasions.

My parents, Louis and Rita, who gave me much needed encouragement and assistance along the way.

Bob Dezelin, a tireless worker and lover of commemorative coins. He suggested several improvements to the mint state frequencies. In addition, he provided an almost spiritual guidance to me the last few months of the project. His tremendous enthusiasm for the book and its contents never waned, for which I am extremely grateful.

Raymond G. Mercer, Jr., President of Stamford Coin Galleries, my first and best teacher in the art of grading and investing in commemorative coins. His thorough knowledge of commemoratives was an absolute necessity to complete the book.

John R. Pasciuti, who provided me with valuable information about prooflike specimens.

Connie Geisz, who edited the book and made it more readable.

Finally, all my co-workers and friends, particularly Helen Nagy, Marcy Kuczo, Joann Singer, Joan Glazer, John Graham, and Tom Smith, who all gave me tremendous support and encouragement during the long progressions of this book.

Foreword

Twenty-five years after the production of the last U.S. Commemorative Half Dollar, an accurate overview of the entire Commemorative series can finally be made. For not until this point in time have the weights of commercial manipulation and speculative investment been countered by the influences of serious collector interest and long-term investor demand.

Fueled by a furious flurry of production between the years 1934 and 1938, speculation in Commemoratives soon thereafter reached a level that would rival that of Holland's tulip bulbs and make American Beam bottles seem conservative by comparison. For example, a Cincinnati Half Dollar soared to fifteen dollars soon after its release in 1936. In B. Max Mehl's famous Dunham Sale of 1941, a Cincinnati Half brought eight dollars (a Proof 1895 Morgan Dollar brought $7.35). It has taken several generations for Commemoratives to recover from such obvious abuse.

Also, not until this decade, during which plans for other special Commemorative issues have been proposed and dismissed, have collectors regarded Commemoratives as a complete series and, therefore, as collectible as Franklin Halves, Mercury Dimes, etc. It is obvious that serious interest is on the upswing in the historic Commemorative series, while speculation, albeit not completely dispelled, has been reduced to a tolerable level. This trend will no doubt continue.

The international scope of the Commemorative marketplace is a relatively recent, but significant, factor. It seems that foreign collectors and investors, particularly those from Europe and Japan, turn readily to Commemoratives when they consider purchasing coins from the United States. Interest from abroad has on more than one occasion accounted for a movement in Commemorative coin prices.

Because of the maturity of the Commemorative series, and because of the increased emphasis placed on the strict grading of all coins by collectors and investors, the appearance of A Comprehensive Guide is very timely. Its buying tips are indispensable to a prospective purchaser of any U.S. Commemorative coin. Its helpful information is entertaining and educational to the novice or the established collector. Never before has any numismatic work offered such practicality as is offered in this volume.

Steve Ivy

Table of Contents

Preface iii
Acknowledgements iv
Foreword v
Definitions of Terms ix
Introduction 1
Chapter I Why Collect Commemoratives? 3
Chapter II The Need for a Comprehensive Guide 5
Chapter III The Grading Controversy 7
Chapter IV Original Issue Holders 9
Chapter V Toning 11
Chapter VI Grading Silver Commemoratives: A Final Note 13
Chapter VII Investment Potential of Silver Commemoratives 15
Chapter VIII U.S. Silver Commemoratives: A Type-By-Type Analysis 19
    Type-By-Type Analyses:
        Isabella Quarter Dollar 21
        Lafayette Dollar 23
        Alabama Centennial 25
        Albany, New York 27
        Battle of Antietam 28
        Arkansas Centennial 29
        Bay Bridge (San Francisco-Oakland) 31
        Daniel Boone Bicentennial 32
        Bridgeport, Connecticut, Centennial 34
        California Diamond Jubilee 35
        Cincinnati Musical Center 37
        Cleveland, Great Lakes Exposition 39
        Columbia, South Carolina, Sesquicentennial 40
        Columbian Exposition 42
        Connecticut Tercentenary 44
        Delaware Tercentenary 45
        Elgin, Illinois, Centennial 46
        Battle of Gettysburg 48
        Grant Memorial 49
        Grant with Star Memorial 51
        Hawaiian Sesquicentennial 53
        Hudson, New York Sesquicentennial 55
        Huguenot-Walloon Tercentenary 57
        Iowa Centennial 59
        Lexington-Concord Sesquicentennial 60
        Lincoln-Illinois Centennial 61
        Long Island Tercentenary 62
        Lynchburg, Virginia, Sesquicentennial 63
        Maine Centennial 64
        Maryland Tercentenary 66
        Missouri Centennial 67

(Table of Contents continued.)

   Monroe Doctrine Centennial 69
   New Rochelle, New York 71
   Norfolk, Virginia, Bicentennial 73
   Oregon Trail Memorial 74
   Panama-Pacific Exposition 76
   Pilgrim Tercentenary 78
   Rhode Island (Providence) Tercentenary 80
   Roanoke Island, North Carolina 82
   Robinson-Arkansas Centennial 83
   San Diego, California-Pacific Exposition 84
   Sesquicentennial of American Independence 85
   Old Spanish Trail 87
   Stone Mountain Memorial 89
   Texas Independence Centennial 90
   Fort Vancouver Centennial 92
   Vermont Sesquicentennial 94
   Booker T. Washington Memorial 95
   Washington-Carver 97
   Wisconsin Territorial Centennial 99
   York County, Maine, Tercentenary 100
Chapter IX Gold Commemoratives 101
Chapter X Investment Potential of Gold Commemoratives 103
Chapter XI U.S. Gold Commemoratives: A Type-By-Type Analysis .. 105
 Type-By-Type Analyses:
   Grant Memorial Dollar 106
   Lewis and Clark Exposition Dollar 107
   Louisiana Purchase Exposition Dollar 109
   McKinley Memorial Dollar 111
   Panama-Pacific Exposition Dollar 112
   Panama-Pacific Exposition Quarter Eagle 113
   Panama-Pacific Exposition Fifty Dollar (Round) 114
   Panama-Pacific Exposition Fifty Dollar (Octagonal) 115
   Sesquicentennial of American Independence Quarter Eagle ... 116
Chapter XII 1979: The Year of the Commemorative? 117
Chapter XIII Statistical Table for U.S. Silver Commemoratives 119
Chapter XIV Statistical Table for U.S. Gold Commemoratives 123
Chapter XV Important Grading Highlights for Silver Commemoratives ... 125
Chapter XVI A Chronology of Commemorative Coinage 127
Chapter XVII Recommended Reading 129

Definitions of Terms

Abrasion-Can appear on mint state or circulated pieces. The term, as it is used in A Comprehensive Guide, refers to friction which sometimes appears on an uncirculated coin's surface. The friction is a result of mint state pieces coming into contact with one another in original rolls or bags.

Ask-The wholesale price a dealer requests another dealer to pay for a coin.

AU-Abbreviation for Almost Uncirculated. Refers to a coin which has circulated slightly and retains most of its original luster.

Average Unc-MS60. (See Chapter III for details.)

Bag Mark-A surface mark on a coin. They are acquired when coins come into contact with one another in a mint sewn bag. Generally, the larger the coin (e.g. half dollar, silver dollar) the more severe are the marks, or cuts, on the coin.

Bid-The wholesale price a dealer will generally pay another dealer for a coin.

BU-Abbreviation for Brilliant Uncirculated. Refers to a coin which has not circulated and retains its original luster. As the term is generally used today, BU also refers to an MS60 specimen.

Cleaning Merchant-An unscrupulous coin dealer who cleans circulated coins and attempts to sell them as mint state specimens.

Detracting Mark-Refers to a scuff mark, bag mark, abrasion, etc., which is located in a prominent position on a coin's surface. (See Chapter III for details.)

Devices-The major features on each side of the coin. For example, on the Columbian Half Dollar, Columbus' head on the obverse and the sailing ship on the reverse.

Field-The flat portion of a coin's surface which does not have a design or inscription.

Gem BU-MS65. (See Chapter III for details.)

Greysheet-The coin industry's term for the Coin Dealer Newsletter, which is printed on grey paper.

Handling Mark-Refers to coin marks which are a result of improper handling. In many instances, it may be impossible to differentiate a bag mark from a handling mark.

Hairlines-Tiny lines or scratches caused by polishing or improper cleaning of a coin. They are most visible on the fields.

Luster-The mint bloom ("frost") on the surface of an uncirculated coin. It can range from brilliant to dull in appearance. Once a coin has circulated or been improperly cleaned the natural luster cannot be restored.

Mint Bloom-See luster.

Mint Mark-A small letter used to designate at which mint a coin was struck. For commemoratives, a coin struck at the Philadelphia Mint will not have a mint mark. Coins struck at the Denver Mint will have a "D" and those coined at the San Francisco Mint will exhibit an "S" (except for the 1925 Fort Vancouver Half Dollars, which had the "S" mint mark omitted).

Mint State-Refers to a coin which has not circulated and does not exhibit any sign of wear. The coin may be in MS60, MS65, or MS65+ condition.

Obverse-The front side of a coin. Usually the side with the principal design.

Original Roll-Twenty uncirculated half dollars which were put away during the commemorative year of issue.

Patina-See Toning.

PDS Set-A year set of three commemorative half dollars; one from each mint, Philadelphia, Denver, and San Francisco.

Planchet-The blank metal disc on which a coin design is produced.

Proof-A coin struck from specially polished and prepared dies. The finished coin, sold to collectors at a premium, will exhibit a mirror-like surface.

Prooflike-An uncirculated coin with proof surfaces. Some coins exhibit deep, reflective surfaces while others are partially prooflike (termed semi-prooflike).

Prooflike, Cameo-A prooflike coin contrasted with frosted silver devices.

Reverse-The back side of a coin. Generally, the side which displays the less important design.

Sandblast Proof-A special type of proof coin, similar to a matte proof's appearance. Produced by blowing fine sand particles against the surface of the planchet.

Sleeper-A coin which is "asleep" or undervalued at current price levels.

Slide Marks-Fine lines across the devices of a coin. The lines are usualy a result of improper storing of a coin in an album with acetate slides. By constantly removing and inserting a coin in its slot the slide can rub against the coin and cause light friction.

Striations-Thin, raised lines on a coin's surface. They are caused by excessive die polishing.

Strike-Refers to the sharpness of a coin's design details. Sharply struck coins are more desirable than weakly struck specimens.

Superb BU-MS65+. (See Chapter III for details.)

Toning-Natural coloring or patina on a coin's surface. (See Chapter VI for more details).

Unc-Abbreviation for Uncirculated. (See definition for BU.)

Whizzing-An artificial treatment of a coin surface, usually by wire brushing, buffing, or using acid or some abrasive, to make it appear to be in better condition than it is.

Introduction

1892. With the issuance of the Columbian Exposition Half Dollar the collecting of U.S. silver commemorative coins began. From 1892 until 1954, commemorative issues included 142 half dollars of 48 types, one silver dollar, one quarter dollar, five gold dollars, two quarter eagles, and two fifty dollar gold pieces. Each coin was minted as legal tender with the standard size, weight, and fineness for coins of their respective denominations.

All commemorative coins were authorized by Congress and coined at face value. They were sold to the sponsoring groups or commissions at face value; the commissions, in turn, sold the coins at different premiums to coin dealers or the general public. The profits realized by the sponsoring groups were used for the purposes stated in the authorizing legislation.

Oftentimes, not all the commemoratives could be sold by the various commissions. As a result, the remaining coins were returned to the Treasury to be melted.

CHAPTER I
WHY COLLECT COMMEMORATIVES?

Putting together a collection of these coins can be one of the most fascinating and financially rewarding realms of numismatics today. What other coin collection can exhibit fifty-nine different coins, each commemorating a famous (or obscure) person, place, or event? Some collectors look upon their collection as art, others see it as part of our history, while many more collect commemoratives strictly for investment purposes. The person who can combine all three interests is a rare breed of collector.

The collector of U.S. commemoratives today practically has the field all to himself. There are probably only a few hundred serious collectors of these coins throughout the entire country. Each year more and more collectors and investors are being attracted to this challenging area of coin collecting. Each coin is different, each issue has an interesting story to tell, and many pieces have exciting investment potential.

CHAPTER II
THE NEED FOR A COMPREHENSIVE GUIDE

The author has often discussed with other collectors and dealers the pressing need for a grading guide for uncirculated commemoratives. "Is it Average Uncirculated, Gem BU, or Superb BU?" is a question often asked by collectors as well as dealers. One person's Gem BU can be another's Unc, or even AU! This disparity in grading exists not only because of dishonesty on the part of some sellers but also because of a general lack of knowledge on the part of sellers and buyers.

Each commemorative coin type differs from the other fifty-eight types. In a sense, each coin has a personality all its own and will differ from the others in many ways: strike, wear points, surface peculiarities, luster, severity of bag marks and abrasion, and so on. Some coins are easy to find in MS65 condition (Gem BU) or MS65+ condition (Superb BU) while others should be considered rarities in these conditions.

The general lack of information about U.S. commemoratives has led many people to believe it is easy to acquire a complete set of gem or superb commemoratives. It all depends, however, on one's definition of gem or superb! Because each and every coin is different, it can take months, probably years, to acquire the expertise to grade all fifty-nine types and all one hundred and fifty-three pieces which comprise a complete set.

Since both collectors and dealers are becoming increasingly quality conscious, grading standards are becoming more and more strict. A coin which may have been called Superb BU five years ago may only be graded Gem BU today. As coins become more expensive to acquire the public should expect this trend to continue. A Comprehensive Guide takes a very conservative approach to grading U.S. commemoratives. This is the only one to take because when the collector tries to sell his collection he can certainly count on the buyer grading conservatively!

It is all important to the collector, investor, and dealer, therefore, to know the characteristics of a gem or superb coin for each commemorative type before he buys another "gem" or "superb" coin. The author wishes he had a dollar for every commemorative coin which is graded Gem BU or Superb BU but in reality is not!

The primary emphasis of this book is the proper grading of mint state U.S. commemoratives; is the coin MS60 (Average Unc), MS65 (Gem BU), or MS65+ (Superb BU)? The type-by-type analyses will point out those issues which are truly scarce, rare, and underrated in MS65 or MS65+ condition. An important feature in each analysis is the Mint State Frequency scale; the approximate percentage of mint state coins which remain in MS60, MS65 and MS65+ condition for each type.

In addition, the peculiarities of each type with regard to the typical strike encountered, and surface and luster differences are discussed at length.

No book has ever attempted to define, except in broad general terms, what constitutes an MS60, MS65 or MS65+ commemorative type coin. A Comprehensive Guide, however, has undertaken this task; it is a grading guide for uncirculated pieces. With careful study of the different coin "personalities" discussed in each type coin analysis the collector can save hundreds, perhaps thousands, of dollars by purchasing properly graded coins. Happy collecting!

CHAPTER III
THE GRADING CONTROVERSY

The grading debate rages on in numismatic circles. Nothing can be worse for a collector or investor than to purchase a "Gem BU" coin for $100, watch it rise in price to $250 in five years, and, when trying to sell it at a nice profit, find the coin is only AU! If lucky he may get his money back at AU prices but, more likely, this great hobby of numismatics has lost another disillusioned collector forever.

A Comprehensive Guide is written for the collector who has some basic knowledge of numismatics. If you do not know how to differentiate between an uncirculated coin and a coin which is AU then you are looking for trouble (and you will probably find it). If you do not want to learn how to grade and are willing to give your money blindly to a dealer, hope and pray your dealer knows how to grade commemoratives!

This author firmly believes it is foolhardy to spend your hard earned money on coins without, at the very least, having basic knowledge about grading coins. Common sense should tell you this; however, an incredible number of collectors spend hundreds, even thousands, of dollars on coins that are grossly overgraded.

As mentioned previously, there is a trend today towards more conservative grading of uncirculated coins. Because coins, in general, are so expensive, collectors are closely scrutinizing their purchases. In addition, the numismatic press has published numerous articles on the evils of overgraded coins. This has cautioned many people to be on the alert when buying any coin. As a result, most dealers and collectors have tightened their grading standards. This makes a great deal of sense because if an MS60 coin, for example, sells for $80 and the same coin in MS65 condition sells for $120 the collector should expect the coin to be gem, not borderline gem. Grading is both a science and an art, and there will always be differences of opinion between buyer and seller; however, the more knowledge the collector can gather on the subject of grading the better off he will be in the long run.

This book uses the following grading standards for U.S. commemoratives:

MS60 (Average Uncirculated) — A mint state coin which has no wear or "rub" from circulation. It will typically exhibit noticeable abrasion, bag marks, and bruises from being in bags and rolls. In addition, the coin's luster may be unappealing and it may be poorly struck. The majority of mint state coins fit into this category.

MS65 (Gem BU) — A mint state coin which is far above average: pleasing luster, a better than average strike (it can be fully struck), no detracting marks, and no noticeable abrasion. It is, by definition, Gem! Many coins which are labeled "Gem BU", "MS65" are, unfortunately, only Average Unc. (MS60) or almost uncirculated.

This writer has found most serious commemorative collectors and dealers will not grade a coin MS65 if it has a few minor, yet detracting, marks on the obverse. For example, a mint state Alabama can have a virtually flawless reverse, but if the obverse is a bit too "scruffy" on Governor Kilby's cheekbone, the collector or dealer will generally reject the coin as MS65. (An analogy can be drawn here. Not many serious collectors of Morgan Dollars will purchase a Morgan Dollar as MS65 if the reverse is beautiful yet the obverse has some minor, yet noticeable, detracting marks or abrasion on Liberty's cheek.)

MS65+ (Superb BU) — A mint state coin in superb condition: virtually flawless, 90%-100% fully struck, full mint bloom, and no detracting marks or abrasion. This grade coin is the very best obtainable for the coin type. Probably no more than 5% to 10% of all mint state coins deserve this grade. It is a grade widely used but one which seldom fits a coin's actual condition.

MS70 (Perfect Gem BU) — A mint state coin which is absolute perfection, flawless. It is an ideal: full strike, perfect luster, no marks of any kind, etc.

These are general definitions and the book goes into much greater detail for each commemorative coin type. Remember, putting together a set of U.S. commemoratives is not the same as assembling a set of Washington Quarters or Roosevelt Dimes. Read each page carefully and then visit coin shows and coin shops and study the actual coin type carefully. Look at several coins of the same type before purchasing any. Do not buy the first commemorative that looks halfway decent; a gem might be the next coin you look at or the tenth. By looking at several coins with the same design you will become familiar with the characteristics of each coin. All it takes is patience and perserverance and the ability to say "no thank you" when a coin is not really as nice as the seller says it is.

Before buying any coin take it out of its holder (CAREFULLY) and hold it between the thumb and forefinger at the edges. Look at it under a good light with a strong magnifying glass and tip the coin while simultaneously rotating it 360 degrees. By using this method, a defect which does not appear from one angle may appear from another. If the seller does not let you inspect the coin this way do not buy it — there is probably something wrong with it. (The dealer may be afraid you will drop the coin; however, always hold the coin over a soft fabric like velvet to avoid any bruises which would result from accidentally dropping the coin.)

Let the coin, not the holder, describe itself. Some sellers like to "push" or stretch the grade — an uncirculated coin becomes gem, a gem coin becomes superb, etc. If the coin holder describes the coin as "Gem BU" but the coin's characteristics define the piece as "Average Unc" do not pay the gem premium price; you are not buying the holder. YOU ARE BUYING THE COIN! A $50 coin does not become a $100 coin just because the holder says "Gem BU". Use your good judgement and make sure you have a lot of experience in grading these coins. Do not let yourself be pressured into a deal.

Two other factors should send warning signals to the collector. If, for example, a coin normally wholesales for $100 in MS65 condition and you see the same coin being sold for $50 in the "same" condition, the coin is probably overgraded. Why would the seller waste his time and money keeping this coin in stock or advertising it when he could sell it to most dealers for twice the price? The answer lies in the coin's true grade — it probably has been processed or "whizzed" to make it appear better than it actually is. A subscription to a national dealer-to-dealer wholesale price sheet will alert you to these price disparities.

Secondly, if you have any doubt about the coin being the grade it is claimed to be DO NOT BUY IT. First instincts are usually reliable. You will occasionally miss out on a good buy but it is better to be safe than sorry with an overgraded coin. Remember, when it is time to sell the coin to someone else the chances are that any doubts you have about the coin will be magnified to a greater degree by the potential purchaser.

CHAPTER IV
ORIGINAL ISSUE HOLDERS

Many of the commemoratives were distributed in special issue holders. Most of these holders were made of cardboard with inserts for a number of coins, usually three or five. Some commemoratives were issued in individual envelopes, wooden boxes, and even cardboard boxes.

Collecting nice mint state specimens in these holders is a specialized field. Unfortunately, there are many holders on the market which have been damaged, e.g. torn edges, ripped coin tabs, holders written on, etc. Commemoratives in damaged holders are worth little or no premium. However, premium quality (MS65, MS65+) coins in "mint quality" crisp original issue holders often bring premiums of 10%-40% over similar condition coins which do not have holders.

Many coins which have remained in the cardboard holders will display spectacular toning. Others will have toning which is not too attractive. The type of toning is dependent on the chemicals (usually sulfur) in the paper reacting differently with each coin surface. Toning "tab marks" on one side of the coin are usually a good indication the piece came from an original cardboard issue holder.

Before purchasing any commemorative in the original issue holder, inspect it carefully. Check each coin for contact marks, signs of abuse, and fine lines similar to coin album slide marks. These recessed lines occur from improperly removing a coin from underneath a coin tab. After purchasing, carefully store the coins so they do not dislodge from the tabs and come into contact with another coin or a hard surface.

Many opportunities abound for the enterprising numismatist who attempts to collect commemoratives in the original issue holders. For investment purposes, concentrate only on strictly graded MS65 or MS65+ specimens in undamaged holders. It is much more sensible to buy a beautiful commemorative without an original issue holder than to settle for an MS60 (Average Unc.) coin just because it has the holder!

CHAPTER V
TONING

Natural toning, or patina, on the surfaces of a coin usually takes years to develop. For instance, some of the most beautifully toned commemoratives were stored in the old brown Meghrig coin albums. Gorgeous hues and "splashes" of toning on a gem or superb commemorative can make the coin doubly desirably to the collecting connoisseur. However, should the collector pay twice the normal price for such a specimen? For example, is a rainbow toned MS65 Connecticut Half Dollar worth $300? How about $950 for an Isabella Quarter? Only the collector can decide if his budget can afford the premium.

Before paying tomorrow's prices today, the collector should be aware that very few dealers will pay more than a 10% or 20% premium for a nicely toned specimen. While auction records are sometimes established for toned commemoratives one should not compare this market for selling, with a 10% or 20% seller's commission, to the usual and quicker way of selling directly to a dealer.

Paying a high premium of 50% to 100% will probably force the collector or investor to hold on to the coin an additional year or two before a nice return on the investment begins to materialize.

The collecting quality craze is just now beginning to spread to the commemorative series. It was only a year or two ago that the commemorative collector could purchase nicely toned pieces for little or no additional premium!

At the present, a premium of 10% to 30% appears to be reasonable for original and attractively toned MS65 or MS65+ specimens. What will tomorrow bring? Only time will tell.

CHAPTER VI
GRADING SILVER COMMEMORATIVES: A FINAL NOTE

Since most commemoratives did not circulate like normal trade coins, when one grades "commems" the key factor is usually mishandling. Some coins may exhibit abuse or wear at other than the high points of the coins because of the way they were handled by different people. In addition, many coins, particularly the issues minted before 1934, suffered abuse over the years because of the general poor preservation or excessive cleaning by the non-collecting public.

Since so few of these coins have seen actual circulation and do not exhibit wear according to the conventional numismatic definition, it is the author's opinion that learning how to detect an abrasively cleaned commemorative is more important than looking for conventional wear on these coins. (Heavily cleaned Unc. commems should be considered AU.) The collector, if he wants to get the most for his money, must learn to distinguish a natural coin surface from a processed or cleaned surface.

The general myth about commemoratives is they are all readily available in MS65 or MS65+ condition. This is not the case for about one-third of the issues! Unfortunately, when a dealer locates a scarce commem which has not been mishandled or finds a coin which is just a little bit nicer than the average MS60 specimen, the coin is too often automatically graded MS65 or MS65+.

This overgrading is a particular problem with the following type coins; Isabella Quarter, Lafayette Dollar, and the Alabama, Cincinnati, Grant, Hawaiian, Hudson, Maine, Missouri, Monroe, Panama-Pacific, Sesquicentennial, Fort Vancouver, Booker T. Washington, and Washington-Carver Half Dollars. These issues range from scarce to rare in MS65 condition. Most of the available specimens of these type coins on today's market will grade at best, between MS60 and MS65: MS60+.

Only experience in grading the individual issues can prevent you, the collector, from purchasing overgraded and overpriced coins. Remember, each commem type has its own "personality" and will differ from the other forty-nine types. To make valid grading judgements each coin must be graded against coins of the same type. Comparisons must be made with regard to the differences in strike, surface peculiarities, luster, and severity of marks and abrasion. The world's finest mint state Sesquicentennial Half Dollar will not be as eye-appealing to the uninitiated as an MS65 Antietam, Oregon Trail, or Norfolk. An MS65 Alabama will not impress the novice collector like an MS65 Cleveland. However, to the trained eye of the experienced commem collector an MS65 Alabama will be a great addition to his collection!

CHAPTER VII
INVESTMENT POTENTIAL OF SILVER COMMEMORATIVES

	50 Piece Type Set	144 Piece Set
1970:	$2,927.00	$5,922.50
1979:	$14,602.75	$28,343.50
Appreciation:	399%	379%

As one can see from the above prices for a 50 piece type set and a complete 144 piece set, as an investment the silver commemoratives have done very well the past few years. (The 50 piece set's price was obtained by adding the retail price of each "type" coin; in the case of two coins of the same type, e.g. the 1920 and 1921 Pilgrim, the lower priced coin was used. The 144 piece set's price was obtained by adding the individual retail prices of all the issues: both single coins and PDS sets.)

Recently many professional numismatists have extolled the investment potential of various coin series. Many of these series have indeed shown fantastic price increases for gem and superb specimens; e.g. type gold, Mercury dimes, Barber coins, Seated Liberty coins, Standing Liberty quarters, Walking Liberty half dollars — the list goes on and on. Price increases of 200%, 300%, even 400% have not been uncommon for many issues in these series. Silver commemoratives, however, while performing very well since 1970, have been relatively dormant the past three years. Only a very few issues (e.g. Isabella, Lafayette) have shown excellent price advances.

Despite the fact many of the individual issues have done very well the past nine years, most of the silver commemoratives still have tremendous investment potential and the series, on the whole, is one of the last untapped investment areas of numismatics. Many issues show promise for short term (1-2 years) profits while others will certainly be excellent long term (3-5 years) bets for strong upward price appreciation.

A note of caution must be expressed at this time. Most coin investments should be held a minimum of three years. Do not commit your rent money in the hope you will double your money in two months! Collector and investor demand for different coin series runs in cycles. A particular coin series can lay dormant for years while collectors and investors concentrate their interests elsewhere. However, when they begin concentrating on a particular series, prices can increase dramatically in just a short time. If one spends countless hours in studying the coin market each week one might be able to speculate short term by anticipation of an upswing in a particular series. However, this sort of short term speculating is just that — speculation — your timing may be poor and if you need your money fast you can often lose 10% to 30% of your investment because you have to liquidate at the wrong time. Therefore, it is imperative any money spent investing in coins be done with money you can afford to tie up for the long term so that the coins can be sold when they are in the greatest demand and not when you are desperate for money. When a coin series is "hot" coin dealers will often throw away the book to buy gem and superb BU coins. However, when there is little demand for a particular coin and you are forced into a quick sale because of a need for cash you could very well get hurt financially.

In addition, the time to buy coins is not when the series is hot and showing price increases every week, but when it is dormant. Many dealers will gladly sell nice material at lower than usual prices if there is no particular demand for the coin at that time. So, when buying coins in a series which is being ignored by others, negotiate hard and you will save some money. Beware of overgraded "bargains" which are always around — know the difference between a gem coin that is a bargain and a bargain coin that is not a gem. Learn how to tell the difference!

The U.S. silver commemorative market is still in its infancy. Very few dealers in the country specialize in this series or even regularly stock the coins. In addition this series has only appeared in the weekly *Coin Dealer Newsletter* ("Greysheet") since January 3, 1969, so dealer to dealer activity has been monitored for a little more than ten years.

There are many reasons why this author feels many of the silver commemoratives are excellent long term investments.

1. The mintages are very low. Most mintages of commemorative coins are in the low tens of thousands and the prices are still, comparatively speaking, very low. For example, what other coin series can boast a coin like the 1934 Boone Half Dollar, with a mintage of 10,007, that sells between $80 and $100 in gem and superb BU condition? Considering how conscious many collectors are of mintages it is surprising many of these coins do not sell for much more.

2. Many issues are very beautiful and historically significant. Granted, some issues commemorate rather obscure people, places, and events, but on the whole, the story behind the coins can be just as fascinating as the coin itself. A perfect example is the Oregon Trail Half Dollar; what other coin displays so beautifully the spirit of America?

3. Many issues have been widely distributed to collectors and non-collectors alike. There are very few large hoards on the market to depress the price should they be released. It is difficult to corner the market in these low mintage coins because there are so few of them around in gem condition to begin with.

4. Because many issues have been distributed to non-collectors who did not know how to properly preserve them, many coins have been abused over the years through mishandling, cleaning, or normal circulation. Some examples of this mishandling of coins are the Isabella Quarter, Lafayette Dollar, and the Alabama, Grant, Missouri and Panama-Pacific Half Dollars. Therefore, the supply of gem and superb coins is much lower than the already low mintages indicate.

There is a general misconception among many dealers and collectors that commemoratives are readily available in nice mint state condition. Many advertisements list gem and superb BU commemoratives for sale. However, quite a few of these coins are only Average Uncirculated, or worse yet, circulated! Other dealers advertise coins which they do not have in stock. When they get an order for a particular coin which they do not have, they will "scramble" to find one from another dealer to fill the order. Dealers and collectors who specialize in gem commemoratives know how difficult it is to find really nice pieces. There is a lot of garbage on the market but not as much gem material as the average collector thinks.

5. In addition to many of the issues which have low mintages and are good bets for price appreciation there are many "sleepers" with higher than normal commemorative mintages. Collectors who rely solely on low mintages to determine value tend to overlook coins with higher mintages. However, these people fail to take into account the number which remain in gem or superb BU condition. The Alabama issue is a perfect example. For years the Alabama 2x2, with a mintage of 6,006, sold for almost double the Alabama plain variety, which has a mintage of 59,038. Collectors and dealers overlooked the fact most 2x2's were distributed to numismatists while the plain variety was distributed, for the most part, to the non-collecting public. As a result, most Alabama "plains" have been circulated or abused while many of the 2x2 variety have not; and the remaining supply of both varieties in nice mint state condition is about the same. The price gap between the two varieties is only now narrowing to about equal prices.

6. Because most of the issues can be purchased for moderate 10%-20% premiums over MS65 prices, the purchase of true Superb MS65+ commemoratives is highly recommended today. Five to ten years from now this price differential could dramatically change. One only has to reflect on the type coin market a few years ago to remember buying gem coins for very modest 5% to 10% premiums over Average Uncirculated and BU prices. How times have changed! Superb type coins are bringing fantastic premiums at auction and over the counter — as much as 100% to 300%! While the author does not want to imply the same thing will occur in the commemorative coin series for Superb BU specimens, the trend should follow, perhaps on a lesser scale. The very scarce issues

should show the most dramatic price advances for superb specimens in the future because the supply is extremely limited. Furthermore, however the commemorative market may be doing at any particular time, there is always demand for strict Superb BU scarce commemoratives. No matter how the market is performing, they are the cream of the crop and very difficult to locate.

While commemoratives appear to be excellent long term investments there are other factors which may depress some of the issues and retard their otherwise excellent profit potential. These factors are outlined below.

1. When determining a value for anything supply and demand come into play. If demand is high and supply cannot meet demand, the price will rise. However, if the supply of a scarce coin is low, yet the demand is not present the coin will not rise in price. This is an important concept to keep in mind when collecting commemoratives because most collectors today collect commemoratives by type (50 piece set) and not by complete set (144 pieces). A type set consists of one type of each issue, so many collectors will purchase the most common, and cheapest, coin of a particular type. For example, a collector who needs an Oregon Trail Half Dollar for a type set will often buy the rather plentiful and cheaper 1926 or 1926-S dates and ignore the much scarcer 1928, 1933-D, 1934-D, 1936, 1936-S or 1937-D coins. These scarcer, and much lower mintage issues, often go unnoticed and demand can remain dormant. The Grant with Star Half Dollar is another good example. Since the Grant (no star) Half Dollar variety sells for about 10% of the star variety a type collector will usually buy the "plain" variety and save a few hundred dollars. In Gem or Superb BU condition the Grant with Star is very, very scarce. It has a mintage of less than 4,300 and only a small fraction of these remain in nice mint state conditon, yet demand at the present for this coin is not that great. Should collectors and investors begin assembling complete 144 piece sets or start concentrating on the scarcer issues, this situation could change almost overnight.

2. Many commemoratives are advertised and sold today as Gem BU and Superb BU at bargain prices. These artificially low prices have tended to depress the true values of properly graded coins. They have also created the false impression to the public that commemoratives in these conditions are easy to buy. Commemoratives which are called "Gem" or "Superb" are easy to buy. Coins which truly grade Gem BU or Superb BU are not that plentiful. Until people take the time to learn how to differentiate between an AU, Average Uncirculated, Gem BU, and Superb BU commemorative these "merchants" will always be around to prey on the unsuspecting collector. One way to help to determine whether a particular commemorative's price is too good to be true is to subscribe to the *Coin Dealer Newsletter*. This informative newsletter reports the national coin market on a weekly basis. It reports dealer to dealer wholesale Bid and Ask prices for Average Uncirclated (MS60) and Gem BU (MS65) commemoratives, as well as for circulated (XF/AU) commemoratives. If you see a commemorative coin which legitimately wholesales for $100 and is advertised for $60 do not waste your time on the coin — it has to be overgraded or the dealer would sell it to another dealer. It is common sense! If your local dealer cannot get along without his "greysheet", how can you as a collector or investor?

3. From time to time commemoratives are subject to promotion by dealers. Occasionally one or two dealers will try to promote an issue or two (or the entire series) on the nationwide teletype network to try to make a quick profit on coins which they already have in stock. Beware of rapid price advances in any issue. This is usually a good indication a coin is being promoted. (It may also be a good time for the astute investor to sell!) Look for steady, slower price advances because these increases will more than likely endure whereas quick, spectacular advances are often followed by profit taking and sharp price declines.

The 1973 commemorative coin market is an excellent illustration of rapid price advances followed by equally rapid price declines. For example, the Hawaiian Half Dollar sold for about $700 in early January, 1973. By the end of March, 1973, this same coin was selling for $1,200! However, at the end of the same year this issue had declined to the $700 level. During the same period the 1933-D Oregon Trail sold for $65, $170, and $95 and the 1936-S Oregon Trail sold for $55, $120, and $80. The Cincinnati PDS set sold for approximately $450 in January, 1973. By the end of June, 1973, this set had doubled in price to $900! However, by the end of the same year the set had reached the $600 level. The Columbia, S.C. PDS set followed a similar price pattern during this time; $235, $415, and $255.

CHAPTER VIII
U.S. SILVER COMMEMORATIVES: A TYPE-BY-TYPE ANALYSIS

On the following pages are presented type-by-type analyses of the fifty commemorative issues. In addition, because of the rarity of the Grant with Star variety, a separate analysis is also included for this issue.

The coin illustrations at the top of each page have been enlarged to capture each specimen's detail and surface peculiarities. Each commemorative pictured is in premium quality mint state condition: MS65 or MS65+.

Net Mintage: This figure represents the total collectable coinage (uncirculated and circulated) for each date. In many cases coins remained unsold and were returned to the mints to be melted. In effect, each figure represents the total number of coins minted less the number melted.

MS65 Retail Price Analysis: This section lists the retail prices for MS65 specimens for January, 1970 and January, 1979. Today no coin book should be used as a sole pricing guide because the coin market has become too sophisticated with daily fluctuation in prices usually the rule, and not the exception. Many major coin dealers trade actively over teletype so wholesale prices sometimes change hourly! The "good old days" of relying strictly on a yearly price guide for buying and selling rare coins are forever past.

The prices listed should be used as reference points to determine price trends and, perhaps, forecast future prices. To obtain current price data the collector should subscribe to coin newspapers like COIN WORLD, NUMISMATIC NEWS and to the COIN DEALER NEWSLETTER to get up-to-the-minute retail and wholesale figures. (See Recommended Reading Chapter.) This is particularly important for the person who plans to collect either the 50 piece set ($14,000+) or the 144 piece set ($28,000+).

Mint State Frequency: This scale attempts to approximate the percentage of mint state specimens which can be found in the three grades of uncirculated: MS60 (Average Unc.), MS65 (Gem BU), and MS65+ (Superb BU). Once a collector has determined a certain commemorative type coin is in mint state condition (not an easy task for most collectors) he can then use this scale to determine the odds of it being in MS60, MS65, or MS65+ condition. This scale is for type coins only and should not be used for the scarcer singles or PDS sets.

For example, assume a type coin has the following Mint State Frequency:
   MS60 : 40%
   MS65 : 50%
   MS65+: 10%

This scale would indicate the particular mint state type coin has a 4 in 10 (40%) chance of grading MS60, a 5 in 10 (50%) chance of grading MS65, and only a 1 in 10 (10%) chance of grading MS65+. It must be noted that the many coins which just miss grading MS65 are included in the MS60 column in each analysis.

These percentages were determined by a combination of thorough research of hundreds of legitimate commemorative offerings listed in catalogs, magazines, and newspapers, the author's experience of seven years of commemorative collecting, and the professional expertise of rare coin dealer Raymond G. Mercer, Jr., who has bought and sold hundreds of thousands of dollars worth of commemoratives the past ten years.

One point must be emphasized at this time; commemorative types with equal mint state frequency percentages are not necessarily equal in scarcity. For example, one coin which has a mint state population of 20,000 and an MS65 rating of 50% would have approximately 10,000 pieces remaining in MS65 condition. Another type coin with the same MS65 frequency and an uncirculated population of 40,000 would have about

20,000 pieces left in MS65 condition. Even though both type coins have identical percentage frequencies the first coin is twice as scarce as the second coin in MS65 condition.

This rating simply states the FREQUENCY with which a collector can expect a mint state commemorative type coin to be correctly graded MS60, MS65, or MS65+. It is NOT meant to be used as an investment or price rating by itself.

Typical Mint State Specimen: This section states what the typical mint state specimen will look like; it will be either MS60, MS65, or MS65+. The strike, luster, and surface peculiarities will be noted for the typical grade mint state specimen encountered.

Comments: This section will expand on the proper grading of mint state specimens of each type coin. It will advise the collector which coins are generally overgraded, excessively cleaned, or exhibit signs of circulation. In addition, single coins and varieties, as well as PDS sets, where applicable, will be dicussed in regard to scarcity, demand, and investment potential. Suggested price premiums to pay for gem and superb BU specimens are also included. Finally, the author has singled out some "sleepers" issues or coins which are much scarcer than is generally believed. These coins might be of particular interest to investors.

Buying Tips: This last section places a final emphasis on the proper grading of each type coin; what to look for in particular on each coin before buying it. In addition, for certain issues other comments may be made regarding cleaned specimens, PDS sets, and facts peculiar to that particular type coin.

The collector can use all the features on each page, Mint State Frequency, Net Mintage, MS65 Retail Price Analysis, Typical Mint State Specimen, Comments and Buying Tips to piece together the parts of the collecting or investing puzzle for commemorative coins. A Comprehensive Guide does not make any concerted effort to recommend any specific coins for investment, although, in some instances, the author has expressed his opinion on the relative merits of certain coins. However, the collector or investor, by using this book as a guide, should be able to make sounder judgements when purchasing U.S. silver commemorative coins.

Isabella
Quarter Dollar

Net Mintage
24,214

Mint State Frequency
MS60   :   85%
MS65   :   10%
MS65+ :   5%

MS65 Retail Price Analysis
1970: $ 82.50
1979: $625.00
Appreciation: 658%

Typical Mint State Specimen
MS60: Detracting marks, facial abrasion, general poor preservation, possible light cleaning.

Comments

The 1893 Isabella Quarter, a very difficult coin to locate in Gem MS65 and Superb MS65+ condition, is a sleeper in the silver commemorative coin series.

In general, this issue was sharply struck. Some coins, however, exhibit weakness in the hair detail. Such weakness is due to the striking of the coin or die wear. Many Isabellas have been numismatically abused or have seen circulation; therefore, there is an overabundance of XF/AU pieces on the market. In addition, many of this issue have been buffed and retoned to appear BU. They are readily available to the unwary collector.

Most mint state Isabellas will grade only MS60 (average Unc) because of detracting marks, facial abrasion, light cleaning, or general poor preservation. Coins in this condition should command no more than 60% to 70% of MS65 prices and are not recommended for investment.

The supply of strictly graded MS65 pieces in the numismatic marketplace the past few years has practically disappeared. Purchase of these pieces is recommended for future price appreciation.

MS65+ specimens, which should be virtually flawless, are very scarce and purchase is also recommended for excellent future price increases. A truly superb coin can command a premium of between 25% to 50% more than a gem specimen.

Prooflikes exist but they are extremely scarce. Beware of superb prooflikes which are sometimes sold as proofs. (There were reportedly 100 proof Isabellas made, but very few survive today; be very careful. A true proof can sell for over $1,500.) Gem and superb prooflikes can sell for as much as 100% more than normal luster pieces.

Buying Tips
When purchasing a mint state Isabella Quarter inspect the cheekbone and strand of wool for signs of wear.

An MS65 specimen should be sharply struck. In addition, it should be free of slide marks, facial problems, and detracting marks. Make sure the coin exhibits full, original mint bloom.

Many specimens have suffered from numismatic cleaning over the years; be certain the coin has not been a victim of this abuse.

Lafayette
Dollar

Net Mintage
36,026

Mint State Frequency
MS60 :   90%
MS65 :   9%
MS65+:   1%

MS65 Retail Price Analysis
1970: $ 195.00
1979:   3,750.00
Appreciation: 1823%

Typical Mint State Specimen
MS60: Poorly struck, heavy bag marks, facial abrasion, dull luster, general poor preservation, possible light cleaning.

Comments
The 1900 Lafayette Dollar is probably the rarest commemorative coin to locate in Gem MS65 or Superb MS65+ condition. Many of this issue have been abused or have seen circulation; the majority grade XF/AU. Beware of coins which have been buffed and retoned to appear BU. They are readily available to the novice purchaser.

Most mint state Lafayettes will grade only MS60 because of dull luster, heavy bag marks, facial abrasion, and a general poor strike. Some specimens may even be a victim of light cleaning. MS60 specimens should sell for no more than 40% to 50% of MS65 prices.

In MS65 condition this coin is very scarce and should continue its excellent price appreciation. In MS65+ condition this coin is rare and purchase is strongly recommended. Probably no more than 100 pieces exist in this ultimate condition. A collector or dealer who owns such a coin can literally "name his price" when selling a superb Lafayette!

Buying Tips
When purchasing a mint state Lafayette Dollar inspect Washington's cheekbone on the obverse and Lafayette's left shoulder and the horse's head and left rear leg on the reverse for signs of wear.

Before buying an MS65 or MS65+ Lafayette Dollar pay particular attention to the coin's luster. It should have its original mint bloom; or, if the piece is toned, the toning should be natural with depth and iridescence. Examine the facial area of Washington and Lafayette: it should be free of slide marks and exhibit no noticeable abrasion. In addition, the piece should be well struck and be without any detracting bag marks.

Beware of prooflike Lafayettes; counterfeits exist. The author has never seen a genuine, full prooflike Lafayette Dollar.

One should not be overly concerned with the idea of acquiring a coin with a "full boot". Some consider a full boot to mean a separation between the top of Lafayette's boot and his leg. The author considers a full boot to mean a full, rounded boot. However, when grading this coin, one must study the entire surface and features. To enhance an inferior coin's saleability, unscrupulous sellers have been known to re-engrave the boot to attract a buyer with "full boot mania". It is better to buy a specimen which grades MS65 in every respect than to purchase a piece which is inferior in quality just because it has a full boot.

Alabama Centennial
Half Dollar

Net Mintage
    2X2 variety: 6,006
    Plain variety: 59,038

Mint State Frequency
    MS60 :   85%
    MS65 :   10%
    MS65+:   5%

MS65 Retail Price Analysis

	2X2	Plain
1970:	$ 72.50	$ 52.50
1979:	600.00	465.00
Appreciation:	728%	786%

Typical Mint State Specimen
    MS60: Weakly struck, poor luster, excessive bag marks, facial abrasion, general poor preservation.

Comments

The 1921 Alabama Half Dollar (both varieties) is one of the real sleepers in the silver commemorative coin series. It is much more difficult to locate in Gem MS65 or Superb MS65+ condition than is generally believed.

Most Alabamas have circulated to some degree or have undergone some numismatic abuse over the years. Beware of coins which have been buffed and are presented as BU; they are plentiful on the numismatic market.

The vast majority of the few thousand surviving mint state Alabamas grade only MS60 because of numerous problems: weak strike, poor luster, excessive bag marks, and facial abrasion running horizontally across Governor Kilby's face. (Tip and rotate the coin in light and the lines will usually appear.)

Many mint state Alabamas exhibit poor detail on the eagle's feathers and claws on the reverse of the coin. However, some tolerance for weakness of strike, particularly on the coin's reverse, should be made when grading the piece MS65 because most specimens were poorly struck. (The author has seen very few fully struck Alabamas.) But noticeable facial abrasion on the obverse will downgrade the coin to MS60.

Purchase of MS60 Alabamas is not recommended for investment because the coins in this grade are very unattractive. Coins in this grade are considerably less valuable than MS65 specimens because, in addition to being very unappealing, they are quite plentiful in comparison.

MS65 Alabamas are scarce and purchase is recommended. MS65+ specimens are very scarce and purchase is strongly recommended. Such coins can command a 30% to 50% premium over gem pieces. Many gem and superb specimens exhibit brilliant, frosty luster on the reverses while the obverses often have subdued luster.

Some debate exists about the relative scarcity of the two varieties in MS65 or MS65+ condition. The 2X2 variety has a total net mintage of about one-tenth of the plain variety. However, very few of the higher mintage plain variety were preserved properly. In the past, the plain sold for 60% to 70% of the 2x2's price. But in recent months it has been selling at about 70% to 80% to the 2X2's price. The future will probably find both selling at comparable prices in gem and superb condition.

Buying Tips

When purchasing a mint state Alabama Half Dollar inspect Governor Kilby's cheekbone and the eagle's breast for signs of wear.

An MS65 specimen should not exhibit any noticeable facial abrasion or slide marks. Make sure the coin is sharply struck, possesses its original mint bloom, does not have unsightly bag marks, and has not been cleaned.

An MS65+ specimen, which will prove to be very difficult to find, should be as problem free as possible: no detracting marks, no facial abrasion, at least 90% fully struck, and full, frosty mint bloom.

Albany, New York
Half Dollar

Net Mintage
  17,671

Mint State Frequency
  MS60 : 30%
  MS65 : 50%
  MS65+: 20%

MS65 Retail Price Analysis
  1970: $ 55.00
  1979: 185.00
  Appreciation: 236%

Typical Mint State Specimen
  MS65: Full mint bloom, minimum marks, little abrasion.

Comments

The 1936 Albany Half Dollar, despite its relatively low mintage, can be obtained in Gem MS65 condition without much difficulty. About one-half of all mint state pieces can be graded MS65.

The average MS60 specimen will exhibit numerous handling marks, particularly on the beaver on the obverse and on the two men on the reverse; in addition, look for slide marks and abrasion on the beaver's hip. Coins which have these problems cannot be graded MS65 or MS65+.

Because of the relatively plentiful supply of MS65 specimens, MS60 pieces should not be purchased for investment purposes. A Gem specimen costs only about 10% more than an average Unc coin. This is a modest premium to pay to guarantee the coin's resaleability on the numismatic market.

While MS65+ pieces are a bit more difficult to find, they can be purchased for modest premiums of 5% to 15% over MS65 specimens; in the future this grade coin should be in the greatest demand by collectors.

Buying Tips

When purchasing a mint state Albany Half Dollar inspect the beaver's hip and the sleeve of Governor Dongan (man on left) for signs of wear.

Before buying an MS65 or MS65+ specimen pay particular attention to the mint bloom of the coin. Closely examine its obverse for slide marks, excessive marks on the beaver, and abrasion. Also, on the reverse be on the lookout for heavy handling marks on Governor Dongan and Peter Schuyler. Specimens which exhibit these problems should grade MS60.

Battle of Antietam
Half Dollar

Net Mintage
18,028

Mint State Frequency
MS60 : 25%
MS65 : 50%
MS65+: 25%

MS65 Retail Price Analysis
1970: $ 82.50
1979: 250.00
Appreciation: 203%

Typical Mint State Specimen
MS65: Full, frosty mint bloom, minimum handling marks.

Comments
The 1937 Antietam Half Dollar, even with a rather low mintage, is available in Gem MS65 condition without much difficulty.

The great majority of Antietams remain in mint state condition and of these about 50% can be graded MS65. Superb MS65+ pieces are not too difficult to find. In fact, the Antietam is one of the easiest low mintage commemoratives to locate in Superb condition.

The fields of all uncirculated coins have a pleasing brilliant, chiseled, "ripple" effect.

MS60 Antietams will generally exhibit marks on the faces of Lee and McClellan on the obverse and over the letters THE BURNSIDE BRIDGE on the reverse.

Since most mint state Antietams can usually be located in nice condition, purchase of lesser quality coins is not recommended for investment. By paying a premium of 10% to 15% for an MS65 or MS65+ coin, the collector will likely discover in future years this grade coin will appreciate much more than the MS60 specimen; and because most serious commemorative coin collectors want only top quality coins, it will be much easier to sell.

Buying Tips
When purchasing a mint state Antietam Half Dollar inspect Lee's cheek and the leaves of the tree on the right for signs of wear.

MS60 pieces will usually exhibit detracting marks on the faces on the obverse and on the reverse over the words THE BURNSIDE BRIDGE. Mint state coins with these problems cannot grade MS65 or MS65+, but are MS60. Purchase of average Unc specimens is not recommended for investment.

An MS65 Antietam will exhibit full mint bloom and minimum marks. An MS65+ coin will be virtually flawless with full, blazing original luster.

Beware of coins which have been cleaned. A cleaned coin will exhibit numerous hairlines; tilt it in the light and the lines will appear.

Arkansas Centennial
Half Dollar

Net Mintage
(Note: The D&S mint marks can be found on the reverse to the right of the date.)
1935 : 13,012	1936 : 9,660	1937 : 5,505	1938 : 3,156	1939 : 2,104	
1935D: 5,505	1936D: 9,660	1937D: 5,505	1938D: 3,155	1939D: 2,104	
1935S: 5,506	1936S: 9,662	1937S: 5,506	1938S: 3,156	1939S: 2,105	

MS65 Retail Price Analysis

	1935PDS	1936PDS	1937PDS	1938PDS	1939PDS	Type
1970:	$ 40.00	$ 40.00	$ 42.50	$ 70.00	$ 325.00	$14.00
1979:	195.00	160.00	205.00	475.00	1,300.00	55.00
Appreciation:	388%	300%	382%	579%	300%	293%

Mint State Frequency (Type Coin Only)
- MS60 : 50%
- MS65 : 40%
- MS65+: 10%

Typical Mint State Specimen (Type Coin Only)
MS60: Weakly struck, dull luster, excessive and deep bag marks, abrasion.

Comments

The Arkansas Half Dollar type coin (1935P, 1936P, D, or S) is easy to locate in Gem MS65 condition. It is moderately difficult to find in Superb MS65+ condition. To acquire an MS65 or MS65+ PDS set will require more searching on the collector's part; many PDS sets often have only one or two gem or superb coins while the other coins in the set are not as nice.

Many mint state Arkansas Half Dollars are unattractive and exhibit a weak strike, excessive bag marks, and poor luster and abrasion on the neck and cheek of Liberty. Uncirculated coins with these problems should not be graded MS65 or MS65+, but are MS60. Purchase of average Unc pieces is not recommended for investment.

Since most collectors today collect commemoratives by type only, demand for the PDS sets at the present is not too great. However, in the future, when more collectors and investors enter the commemorative market place, demand for these sets should increase. To acquire a gem or superb 1938 or 1939 PDS set will prove to be a very difficult task. The other three sets (1935, 1936, and 1937), which have relatively higher mintages, have proven to be excellent investments in the past and this trend should continue in the foreseeable future.

Buying Tips

When purchasing a mint state Arkansas Half Dollar inspect Liberty's cheek and headband and the eagle's head and left wing for signs of wear.

Make sure an MS65 coin has a sharp strike, nice luster, minimum bag marks, and no slide marks or abrasion. (Many Arkansas Half Dollars exhibit weak breast feathers or a poorly struck scroll which dangles from the eagle's beak; some tolerance for this problem should be allowed for the MS65 grade.) Beware of coins which have been excessively cleaned; they are quite plentiful for this type.

Purchasing a gem or superb Arkansas PDS set can prove to be a very frustrating task for the collector, for the quality of the three coins is often not uniform. When buying a PDS set examine each coin exactly as you would a type coin. If one or more coins does not meet the standards for an MS65 coin do not purchase the entire set at MS65 prices. In particular, avoid coins which have the characteristic heavy and deep bag marks. A PDS set's demand and price are lowered greatly by the condition of the worst coin.

Bay Bridge (San Francisco-Oakland)
Half Dollar

Net Mintage
71,424

Mint State Frequency
- MS60 : 40%
- MS65 : 50%
- MS65+: 10%

MS65 Retail Price Analysis
- 1970: $25.00
- 1979: 66.00
- Appreciation: 164%

Typical Mint State Specimen
MS65: Full luster, no abrasion, no detracting marks on grizzly.

Comments

The 1936-S Bay Bridge Half Dollar is a rather easy coin to locate in Gem MS65 or Superb MS65+ condition.

Many mint state specimens exhibit abrasion and excessive handling marks on the bear's body. In addition, some specimens also display dull luster. Mint state coins exhibiting these problems cannot grade MS65 or MS65+; they are simply MS60.

An MS65 coin should have minimum handling marks, nice luster, and no abrasion; in general, it will have a nice overall appearance. An MS65+ specimen, which should be virtually flawless, can now be purchased for a rather modest premium of about 10% to 15% over gem prices. In the future, this grade coin will be in the greatest demand by collectors and investors.

Buying Tips

When purchasing a mint state Bay Bridge Half Dollar inspect the grizzly bear's left shoulder and the clouds over the bridge for signs of wear.

An MS65 or MS65+ specimen should be free of abrasion and slide marks and should have minimum marks and full mint bloom.

Be careful to avoid the abundance of cleaned pieces on the market today. Since the reverse design of the coin tends to hide problems, closely inspect the obverse for evidence of cleaning: a cleaned coin will exhibit hairlines on the bear and on the exposed fields.

Daniel Boone Bicentennial
Half Dollar

Net Mintage
(Note: The D&S mint marks can be found on the reverse to the right of the Indian's left foot.)

1934 :	10,007	1935 :	10,010	1935/sm.34 :	10,008
		1935D:	5,005	1935D/sm.34:	2,003
		1935S :	5,005	1935S/sm.34:	2,004
1936 :	12,012	1937 :	9,810	1938 :	2,100
1936D:	5,005	1937D:	2,506	1938D:	2,100
1936S :	5,006	1937S:	2,506	1938S :	2,100

MS65 Retail Price Analysis

	1934	1935PDS	1935/sm.34 PDS	
1970:	$20.00	$ 48.00	$ 300.00	
1979:	85.00	195.00	1,260.00	
Appreciation:	325%	306%	320%	

	1936PDS	1937PDS	1938PDS	Type
1970:	$ 48.00	$175.00	$ 290.00	$15.00
1979:	168.00	470.00	1,075.00	58.00
Appreciation:	250%	169%	270%	287%

Mint State Frequency (Type Coin Only)		Typical Mint State Specimen (Type Coin Only)
MS60 :	30%	
MS65 :	50%	MS65: Full luster, no detracting
MS65+ :	20%	marks.

Comments

The Boone Half Dollar type coin is one of the easiest commemoratives to locate in Gem MS65 or Superb MS65+ condition. To acquire an MS65 or MS65+ PDS set, however, will require more searching on the collector's part because many PDS sets often have only one or two gem coins while the other coins in the set are not as nice. However, the Boone PDS sets are somewhat easier to acquire in MS65 condition than some other commemorative PDS issues (e.g. Arkansas PDS sets).

Many mint state Boone Half Dollars exhibit excessive bag marks, particularly on Boone's face. These coins will grade only MS60 and are not recommended for purchase as an investment.

For type coins the 1935P/sm.34, 1935P, 1936P, or the 1937P can usually be found in MS65 or MS65+ condition with little difficulty.

The 1934 first year of issue is more difficult than the "type" years to obtain in gem or superb condition because many were abused by non-collectors.

Since most collectors today collect commemoratives by type only, demand for the Boone PDS sets is not great. However, in the future, when more collectors and investors begin to collect the complete 144 piece set, the demand for these sets should increase. The key 1935/sm.34, 1937, and 1938 PDS sets have a total combined set mintage of approximately 6,600. The 1935 and 1936 sets, which have relatively higher mintages, have appreciated well in MS65 and MS65+ condition in the past and they should continue this upward trend in the future.

The Philadelphia issues of the 1935/sm.34 and the 1937 low mintage sets should sell only at type coin prices. Some dealers try to sell them at prices of about one-third of the total set price; however these two coins have much higher mintages than their counterparts from the Denver and San Francisco mints.

Beware of 1935/sm.34 sets which have had mint marks added to the Philadelphia issue coins. Use a high powered glass and study each mint mark or have the coins authenticated.

On some PDS sets the branch mint (D and S) planchets were polished prior to striking of the coins. This polishing created a chrome-like effect on some of the coins and causes the coin's luster not to match the luster of the other coins in the set. This is not unusual and should not adversely affect the value of the set.

Buying Tips

When purchasing a mint state Boone Half Dollar inspect Boone's ear and the Indian's left shoulder for signs of wear.

Be certain an MS65 or MS65+ specimen is sharply struck and has full luster, minimum bag marks, and no slide marks.

When buying a PDS set examine each coin exactly as you would a type coin. If one or more coins does not meet the standards for MS65 do not purchase the entire set at MS65 prices. A PDS set's demand and price are lowered greatly by the condition of the worst coin.

Bridgeport, Connecticut, Centennial
Half Dollar

Net Mintage
25,015

Mint State Frequency
MS60 : 35%
MS65 : 50%
MS65+ : 15%

MS65 Retail Price Analysis
1970: $ 30.00
1979: 103.00
Appreciation: 243%

Typical Mint State Specimen
MS65: Full mint bloom, minimum marks.

Comments
The 1936 Bridgeport Half Dollar, despite a comparatively low mintage, is not a difficult coin to locate in Gem MS65 or Superb MS65+ condition at the present time.

Average Unc specimens usually display numerous bag marks, particularly on Barnum's face on the obverse and the eagle on the reverse. They may also exhibit handling marks which occur from abuse over the years. Because of the relatively plentiful supply of MS65 coins, MS60 pieces with these problems should not be purchased because their resaleability is not good. In addition, an MS65 specimen costs only about 10% more than an MS60 piece. This is a very small premium to pay to guarantee the coin's resaleability in the future.

MS65+ specimens, while more difficult to find, can usually be purchased for a small 10% to 15% premium over MS65 pieces. In the future, this grade coin should be in the greatest demand by collectors.

Buying Tips
When purchasing a mint state Bridgeport Half Dollar inspect Barnum's cheek and the eagle's wingtips for signs of wear.

Examine Barnum's face and the eagle for excessive marks. MS60 pieces with these marks should be avoided since the supply of gem coins is still rather plentiful.

An MS65 specimen will exhibit full mint bloom and only minimum marks. An MS65+ coin should be virtually flawless.

California Diamond Jubilee
Half Dollar

Net Mintage
86,594

Mint State Frequency
MS60 : 40%
MS65 : 50%
MS65+: 10%

MS65 Retail Price Analysis
1970: $ 26.00
1979: 107.50
Appreciation: 313%

Typical Mint State Specimen
MS65: Full luster, minimum bag marks, no abrasion.

Comments
The 1925-S California Half Dollar is not too difficult to find in Gem MS65 condition. A Superb MS65+ specimen, however will prove to be an elusive piece for the discerning numismatist to locate.

Many pieces have been mishandled by non-collectors and some have seen limited circulation; these coins will usually grade XF/AU. Beware of circulated pieces which have been excessively cleaned; many of these specimens are offered as BU at ridiculously low "bargain" prices.

Many mint state California Half Dollars exhibit abrasion on the miner and the grizzly bear. In addition, excessive bag marks often appear on the fields of the coin. Coins with these problems cannot be graded MS65 or MS65+. They are simply MS60.

An MS65 specimen, in addition to having no abrasion and minimum bag marks, often will exhibit a chrome-like luster. This is not unusual and should not detract from the coin's overall appearance or resaleability.

An MS65+ specimen will exhibit beautiful semi-prooflike fields which are often contrasted by frosted devices (miner and grizzly bear). Such a piece presents a spectacular appearance and purchase is strongly recommended at a now surprisingly modest premium of 30% to 50%. Beware of coins which have been buffed to resemble these semi-prooflikes; hairlines will be apparent in the fields. Use a magnifying glass before purchasing the coin because the majority of Californias have the previously mentioned chrome-like luster. Be careful not to confuse raised die polishing marks with recessed cleaning hairlines.

Buying Tips
When purchasing a mint state California Half Dollar inspect the miner's sleeve and the bear's left front shoulder for signs of wear.

An MS65 specimen should have full luster, minimum bag marks, and no abrasion.

An MS65+ specimen should have full, frosted mint bloom on the devices contrasted by beautiful semi-prooflike fields. In addition, it should not have any detracting marks or abrasion. Beware of coins which have been excessively cleaned to resemble these prooflikes; they will exhibit numerous hairlines and will be unnatural in appearance.

Cincinnati Musical Center
Half Dollar

Net Mintage
(Note: The D&S mint marks can be found on the reverse below the date.)
- 1936 : 5,005
- 1936D: 5,005
- 1936S: 5,006

Mint State Frequency (Type Coin Only)
- MS60 : 70%
- MS65 : 20%
- MS65+: 10%

MS65 Retail Price Analysis

	1936PDS	Type
1970:	$ 405.00	$135.00
1979:	1,050.00	330.00
Appreciation:	159%	144%

Typical Mint State Specimen (Type Coin Only)
MS60: Poorly struck, excessive and deep bag marks, abrasion.

Comments

The Cincinnati Half Dollar type coin is quite difficult to locate in Gem MS65 condition. It is very difficult to find in Superb MS65+ condition. To acquire a gem or superb PDS set will be a very difficult task because many sets often have only one or two gem coins while the other coins in the set are not as nice.

Many Cincinnatis have been abused over the years, either through mishandling or cleaning. Beware of coins which have been excessively cleaned and are offered as uncirculated. At best these pieces will grade XF/AU.

Most mint state Cincinnatis were weakly struck, particularly in the hair detail of Foster. (In fact, the coins were so poorly struck the designer's initials, CO, in the field behind Foster's head are virtually invisible.) Excessive and deep bag marks can be found on the fields and on the face of Foster and the Goddess of Music. In addition, this coin is often plagued by severe abrasion across Foster's face and the Goddess' leg. Mint state coins with these problems cannot grade MS65 or MS65+. They are MS60. Purchase of MS60 specimens is not recommended for investment because they are very unattractive and demand is not great for them.

On many Cincinnatis numerous light striations can be found on the fields. These raised lines are not from numismatic cleaning but from the polishing marks on the dies which struck the coins.

In their search for a gem type coin most collectors will discover that the 1936D issue is the best struck and preserved of the three members of a PDS set.

The first two hundred pieces struck at the Philadelphia, Denver and San Francisco mints were placed in specially marked envelopes. The coins, in turn, were put in numbered and notarized black cardboard holders. Each holder has three slots and a single celluloid strip to cover the coins. On the back of each holder is the following notarized statement:

I hereby certify that the Cincinnati Commemorative half dollars in this container were the _____ coins struck at the Philadelphia, Denver, and San Francisco mints and were received from the three mints in separate envelopes so marked.

(Signature of Thomas G. Melish)
President of the Cincinnati
Musical Center Commemorative
Coin Association

In MS65 or MS65+ condition the Cincinnati Half Dollar has two factors in its favor: as a type coin it has a total mintage of just 15,016 and as a single coin from each mint it has a mintage of approximately 5,000.

Buying Tips

When purchasing a mint state Cincinnati Half Dollar inspect Foster's temple and the Goddess' left breast for signs of wear.

Make sure an MS65 specimen has a sharp strike, minimum bag marks, and no slide marks or abrasion. In addition, be certain the coin has not been cleaned; it should possess its original mint bloom.

When buying a PDS set do not pay a premium for a "put together" set. Only pay a premium for similarly toned coins from each mint. In addition, examine each coin in the set exactly as you would a type coin. If one or more coins does not meet the standards for an MS65 specimen do not purchase the entire set at MS65 prices. A PDS set's demand and price are lowered greatly by the condition of the worst coin.

One final note: BEWARE OF COUNTERFEITS! Cincinnati fakes are often superior in quality to genuine pieces, and many have "phoney" bag marks. If in doubt about the coin, have it authenticated or purchase the coin from a reputable dealer who specializes in U.S. commemoratives.

Cleveland, Great Lakes Exposition
Half Dollar

Net Mintage
 50,030

Mint State Frequency
 MS60 : 25%
 MS65 : 50%
 MS65+: 25%

MS65 Retail Price Analysis
 1970: $18.50
 1979: 42.50
 Appreciation: 130%

Typical Mint State Specimen
 MS65: Full mint bloom, minimum bag marks, no abrasion.

Comments

The 1936 Cleveland Half Dollar is quite easy to locate in Gem MS65 condition. It is not too difficult to locate in Superb MS65+ condition. In fact, this is one of the few commemoratives which is still available in original roll quantities.

Many mint state coins have numerous, and sometimes deep, bag marks on Moses Cleaveland's face on the obverse and the compass on the reverse. In addition, this is another issue which is often plagued by abrasion. Uncirculated specimens with these problems cannot be graded MS65 or MS65+. They are simply MS60.

Since the supply of gem Clevelands is quite plentiful at present, purchase of average uncirculated specimens is not recommended for investment. A gem or superb specimen can be purchased for a modest 10% to 20% premium over an average uncirculated piece. This is a small premium to pay to insure the coin's resaleability in the future.

The author has seen Clevelands in their original issue holders which have been notarized, sealed, and assigned numbers from 1 to 200 (designating the first 200 pieces struck). The lowest numbered coin holder seen by the author has been #38.

Buying Tips

When purchasing a mint state Cleveland Half Dollar inspect Cleaveland's cheekbone and the top of the compass for signs of wear.

An MS65 or MS65+ specimen should have full mint bloom, minimum bag marks, and no slide marks or abrasion. MS60 specimens with these problems are not recommended for investment.

Columbia, South Carolina, Sesquicentennial
Half Dollar

Net Mintage
(Note: The D & S mint marks can be found on the obverse below the sword point.)
  1936 :   9,007
  1936D: 8,009
  1936S: 8,007

Mint State Frequency (Type Coin Only)
  MS60 : 25%
  MS65 : 50%
  MS65+ : 25%

MS65 Retail Price Analysis

	1936PDS	Type
1970:	$165.00	$ 55.00
1979:	655.00	205.00
Appreciation:	297%	273%

Typical Mint State Specimen (Type Coin Only)
MS65: Full mint bloom, minimum bag marks.

Comments

The Columbia, South Carolina, Half Dollar type coin can be found at the present time in Gem MS65 or Superb MS65+ condition without too much difficulty. The Columbia PDS sets are easier to acquire in MS65 condition than some other commemorative PDS issues. However, before buying the entire set at MS65 prices, make sure that each coin in the set grades MS65!

MS60 Columbia Half Dollars will typically exhibit excessive bag marks in the exposed fields on the obverse and reverse. Since this type is still available in MS65 or MS65+ condition at a small markup, purchase of lesser quality coins is not recommended. MS65+ specimens can be purchased for a modest 10% to 15% premium and should be bought because these coins will be in the most demand in the future.

On many Columbias the reverses will exhibit poor luster. This is due to the heavily brushed dies which struck the coins and does not affect the coin's grade. When the coins are toned inexperienced collectors often mistake the reverses of these coins for coins which have been cleaned because the toning is lackluster and uneven.

In MS65 or MS65+ condition this issue has two factors in its favor: as a type coin it has a total mintage of 25,023 and as a single coin from each mint it has a mintage between 8,007 and 9,007.

Buying Tips

When purchasing a mint state Columbia, South Carolina, Half Dollar inspect the breasts of Justice and the top of the palmetto tree for signs of wear.

Closely examine the fields for excessive bag marks. Mint state coins with these marks cannot grade MS65 or MS65+; they are merely MS60. Since many coins have been cleaned be sure to buy coins with full mint bloom (particularly inspect the obverse; the reverse will often have poor luster because of the previously mentioned brushed dies which struck this issue.)

Specimens with nice luster and minimum bag marks will grade either MS65 or MS65+. With a little patience on the collector's part, virtually bag mark free examples of this type can be acquired.

When buying PDS sets examine each coin exactly as you would a type coin. If one or more coins does not meet the standards for MS65 do not purchase the entire set at MS65 prices. A PDS set's demand and price are diminished greatly by the condition of the worst coin.

Columbian Exposition
Half Dollar

Net Mintage
1892: 950,000
1893: 1,550,405

Mint State Frequency
MS60 : 60%
MS65 : 30%
MS65+ : 10%

MS65 Retail Price Analysis

	1892	1893
1970:	$ 7.00	$ 5.50
1979:	42.50	42.50
Appreciation:	507%	673%

Typical Mint State Specimen
MS60: Weakly struck, excessive bag marks, abrasion, possible light cleaning.

Comments

The Columbian Half Dollar is a very underrated coin to locate in Gem MS65 condition. In Superb MS65+ condition it is much more difficult to locate than present prices would suggest.

Most Columbians have circulated to one degree or another and can grade anywhere between AG/AU. Many cleaned pieces exist and are sold as BU; be on the lookout for these. They will have numerous hairlines and an unnatural appearance.

Many uncirculated coins were poorly struck, particularly on Columbus' face and hair on the obverse and the mainsail on the reverse. In addition, many exhibit abrasion on this sail and excessive bag marks on both sides of the coin. Mint state pieces with these problems should not be graded MS65 or MS65+; they must be graded MS60.

Gem and superb prooflike pieces are very underrated. The 1892 is at least twice as scarce as the 1893 in prooflike condition. In MS65+ condition these prooflikes are spectacular looking with deep mirrorlike surfaces and cameo frosted devices. Specimens in this condition should command a substantial premium of between 300% to 500% over MS65 pieces which do not have prooflike surfaces. Incidentally, many of these prooflikes have lavender toning; this enhances the beauty of the coin even further. Beware of prooflike specimens being offered for sale as proofs. Some of these prooflikes have been placed in the original proof leather holders. There were only 100 proofs made and very few survive today, so be very careful!

Buying Tips

When purchasing a mint state Columbian Half Dollar inspect Columbus' hair and the ship's mainsail and the right hemisphere for signs of wear.

Make sure an MS65 specimen has a sharp strike, minimum bag marks, full luster and no abrasion or slide marks. An MS65+ specimen should be virtually flawless. A Superb MS65+ prooflike piece will exhibit deep mirrorlike fields and frosted devices.

This issue is a favorite of the "cleaning merchant" who cleans circulated pieces and offers them as "Gem" or "Superb" to the unwary bargain hunter for ridiculously low prices (often 50% to 60% of wholesale prices!). In addition, be alert for the XF and AU pieces which were cleaned years ago and have naturally retoned into a pleasing iridescent toning; such pieces should still sell at normal circulated prices, or perhaps just a bit more.

Connecticut Tercentenary
Half Dollar

Net Mintage
  25,018

Mint State Frequency
  MS60 :   40%
  MS65 :   45%
  MS65+:   15%

MS65 Retail Price Analysis
  1970: $ 50.00
  1979:   185.00
  Appreciation: 270%

Typical Mint State Specimen
  MS65: Sharply struck, no abrasion, minimum bag marks, full luster.

Comments

The 1935 Connecticut Half Dollar is moderately difficult to locate in Gem MS65 or Superb MS65+ condition.

The majority of this mintage is still available in mint state condition. Some specimens were weakly struck on the leaves of the Charter Oak on the obverse and around the perimeter through the words UNITED STATES OF AMERICA and HALF DOLLAR on the reverse. In addition, excessive bag marks and abrasion are often prominent on the eagle on the reverse. Mint state coins with these problems cannot be graded MS65 or MS65+; they are simply MS60.

An MS65 specimen, in addition to having a sharp strike, minimum bag marks, and no abrasion, must have full, unbroken luster. Since wear first appears on the eagle's wing, any break in the luster will indicate rubbing.

An MS65+ coin can now be purchased for a modest 15% to 20% premium over an MS65 piece. Since top quality pieces should be in the greatest demand in the future they ought to be the first purchased by the collector.

Buying Tips

When purchasing a mint state Connecticut Half Dollar inspect the base of the tree and the eagle's wing between the neck and the left leg for signs of wear.

Examine the eagle on the reverse for abrasion and excessive bag marks. Uncirculated coins with these problems cannot be graded MS65 or MS65+. To be graded MS65 the coin should be sharply struck and have minimum bag marks and no abrasion. Also make sure the piece has full mint bloom by closely inspecting the eagle's wing for any broken luster.

Delaware Tercentenary
Half Dollar

Net Mintage
20,993

Mint State Frequency
MS60 : 60%
MS65 : 30%
MS65+: 10%

MS65 Retail Price Analysis
1970: $ 48.00
1979: 145.00
Appreciation: 202%

Typical Mint State Specimen
MS60: Poorly struck, abrasion, excessive bag marks.

Comments
The 1936 Delaware Half Dollar is a difficult coin to find in Gem MS65 condition. In Superb MS65+ condition this issue is very difficult to locate.

While the majority of this issue remains in mint state condition, many pieces will exhibit heavy abrasion on the roof of the church and the lower middle sail of the ship, the Kalmar Nyckel. In addition, quite a few coins were also weakly struck, particularly on the section above the door. Another problem often encountered with this issue is excessive bag marks. Mint state specimens with these characteristics should not grade any better than MS60.

An MS65 specimen should have a sharp strike, minimum bag marks, full luster, and only light abrasion on the lower middle sail of the ship. (The abrasion on this sail is probably due to imperfection of the dies.)

An MS65+ specimen should exhibit virtually no abrasion on the ship's sail. Despite being very difficult to locate, such a coin can now be purchased for a modest premium of 15% to 20% over gem prices. The author has never seen a mint state Delaware Half Dollar without any sail abrasion.

Buying Tips
When purchasing a mint state Delaware Half Dollar inspect the center of the lower middle sail and the area above the church door for signs of wear.

Closely examine the coin for slide marks and excessive bag marks and the lower middle sail of the ship for noticeable abrasion. Uncirculated pieces with these problems should not be graded MS65 or MS65+, but MS60.

An MS65 specimen will be sharply struck, and will exhibit full luster, minimum bag marks, light abrasion on the ship's sail and no slide marks. A Superb MS65+ piece should exhibit hardly any noticeable abrasion on the sail.

Elgin, Illinois, Centennial
Half Dollar

Net Mintage
20,015

Mint State Frequency
MS60 : 40%
MS65 : 45%
MS65+: 15%

MS65 Retail Price Analysis
1970: $ 41.00
1979: 122.00
Appreciation: 198%

Typical Mint State Specimen
MS65: Sharply struck, minimum bag marks, full luster.

Comments

The 1936 Elgin Half Dollar, despite a low mintage, is comparatively plentiful in Gem MS65 condition. In Superb MS65+ condition, this issue is scarce and undervalued.

Almost all Elgins remain in mint state condition today. However, quite a few of these coins have severe bag marks on the cheekbone of the pioneer on the obverse or on the Pioneer Memorial statue on the reverse. In addition, many pieces were very poorly struck, particularly on the faces of the five pioneers on the statue. On some pieces the baby appears to be a blur. Mint state coins with these characteristics should not be graded MS65 or MS65+, but MS60.

An MS65 coin will be sharply struck; most of the facial features of the five pioneers on the statue should be evident. In addition, the coin should exhibit full mint bloom and minimum bag marks.

An MS65+ specimen will exhibit a full strike on the pioneers' features on the reverse. A superb coin can sometimes be purchased for a modest 15% to 20% premium. However, since such an example is very scarce, expect this premium to increase in the future.

All uncirculated Elgins have a satiny luster. Beware of coins which have a brilliant, chrome-like finish; these specimens have been excessively cleaned and should not be purchased as uncirculated.

On the reverse of many mint state Elgins is a die polishing mark which looks like an erasure rub. The mark is located at two o'clock between the "A" of AMERICA and the boy's head. Because this mark was part of the minting process the coin's grade should not be affected. Many sales have been cancelled by purchasers who thought this mark was a defect.

Buying Tips

When purchasing a mint state Elgin Half Dollar inspect the pioneer's cheekbone and the rifleman's shoulder and left hand for signs of wear.

Make sure an MS65 specimen has full mint bloom, minimum bag marks, and no slide marks. Also, it should be sharply struck. An MS65+ specimen, which should be virtually flawless, should be fully struck. Be sure to purchase an Elgin with satiny luster and not the brilliant, polished appearance which results from having been cleaned.

Battle of Gettysburg
Half Dollar

Net Mintage
26,928

Mint State Frequency
MS60 :   45%
MS65 :   45%
MS65+:   10%

MS65 Retail Price Analysis
1970: $ 44.00
1979:   195.00
Appreciation: 343%

Typical Mint State Specimen
MS65: Full mint bloom, minimum bag marks.

Comments
The 1936 Gettysburg Half Dollar is a more difficult coin to locate in Gem MS65 condition than other issues with lower mintages (e.g. Bridgeport, Connecticut, Elgin). It is quite difficult to find in Superb MS65+ condition.

The great majority of this issue still remains in mint state condition and about one-half of these will grade MS65. The one problem which usually plagues this issue is excessive bag marks, particularly on the two soldiers' cheeks and on the two shields. The marks will be more apparent on the Union shield on the left because the surface has less detail to shelter problems. Mint state specimens with these marks should not grade MS65 or MS65+, but MS60.

An MS65 specimen should have minimum bag marks and full mint bloom. An MS65+ piece can be bought now for a modest premium of 15% to 20%; when located it should be purchased because superb specimens will be in the most demand in the future.

Buying Tips
When purchasing a mint state Gettysburg Half Dollar inspect the soldiers' cheekbones and the three intersecting ribbons which bind the fasces. Also examine the coin for excessive bag marks and slide marks. Mint state pieces with these marks should not be graded MS65 or MS65+. An MS65 specimen should exhibit full mint bloom, minimum bag marks, and no slide marks.

Some gem Gettysburgs have spectacular iridescent toning; they should be purchased by the astute collector or investor because their beauty is worth a premium.

Grant Memorial
Half Dollar

Net Mintage
  67,405

Mint State Frequency
  MS60 : 65%
  MS65 : 25%
  MS65+ : 10%

MS65 Retail Price Analysis
  1970: $ 26.00
  1979:   106.00
  Appreciation: 308%

Typical Mint State Specimen
  MS60: Weakly struck, poor luster, excessive bag marks, abrasion, possible light cleaning.

Comments

The 1922 Grant (no star) Half Dollar is not an easy coin to locate in Gem MS65 condition. It is very difficult to find in Superb MS65+ condition.

Most of this issue have been mishandled to some degree and many have seen circulation; these specimens will generally grade XF/AU.

Beware of circulated pieces which have been excessively cleaned and are offered as BU; they will have a very unnatural appearance.

The majority of uncirculated pieces exhibit a weak strike, particularly on Grant's hair and face. In addition, many have poor luster and exhibit detracting marks. Abrasion on Grant's face is another problem which plagues this issue. Mint state coins with these characteristics should not be graded MS65 or MS65+, but MS60.

The reverse of most Grant Half Dollars is usually nice and semi-prooflike. Therefore, when grading a Grant pay particular attention to the coin's obverse.

Most Grants were struck from heavily brushed dies. This gives the surface of each coin a rough, almost steel wool brushed look. Do not confuse these raised die striations with surfaces which have been harshly cleaned. Excessively cleaned Grants are very unattractive. Because of polishing, they will be unnaturally brilliant and will exhibit numerous recessed hairlines.

An MS65 specimen should have minimum bag marks, no facial abrasion, nice luster, and a sharp strike.

An MS65+ piece, which will prove to be very elusive, should be at least 90% fully struck and have full, highlighted luster. A superb specimen can sometimes be purchased at the present for a surprisingly modest 20% to 25% premium. In the future, when more numismatists become aware of the true scarcity of this coin in superb condition, the premium should be much higher.

Buying Tips

When purchasing a mint state Grant Half Dollar inspect Grant's cheek and the leaves on the tree for signs of wear. Pay particular attention to the obverse of the coin because the reverse is usually almost problem free. An MS65 specimen should be sharply struck and have minimum bag marks and no facial abrasion or slide marks. Also it should exhibit better than average luster.

An MS65+ Grant should exhibit full mint bloom and be 90% to 100% fully struck.

Be certain to inspect Grant's features carefully and do not confuse a weak strike for wear. Furthermore, be on the lookout for the readily available cleaned pieces which are offered as BU to the unwary bargain hunters.

Grant with Star Memorial
Half Dollar

Net Mintage
    4,256

Mint State Frequency
MS60 :	90%
MS65 :	8%
MS65+:	2%

MS65 Retail Price Analysis
1970:	$ 125.00
1979:	1,050.00
Appreciation:	740%

Typical Mint State Specimen
MS60: Weakly struck, poor luster, excessive bag marks, abrasion, possible light cleaning.

Comments

The 1922 Grant with Star Half Dollar is the rarest commemorative half dollar in Gem MS65 condition. It is extremely rare in Superb MS65+ condition.

The same problems which plague the plain Grant also plague the star variety. Two points must be reemphasized: this variety also exhibits very poor natural luster and heavy die striations on the obverse fields.

The vast majority of these coins have undergone some numismatic abuse over the years. Excessive cleaning is a particular problem encountered on many Grants with Star. Harshly cleaned coins will display unnatural brilliance and exhibit numerous hairlines.

Probably less than 5% of the entire mintage exists today in MS65 condition. And it is unlikely that more than 10 or 20 pieces exist in true MS65+ condition. With such a limited supply the current price range of $1,000 to $1,500 for a gem or superb piece appears to be low. MS60 pieces, which are not very attractive, are worth considerably less than gem or superb specimens.

There appear to be two reasons why this variety is so reasonably priced at the present. First, all too often MS60, AU, or cleaned pieces are offered to the public as "Gem BU" or "Superb BU" for below market bargain prices. This has, undoubtedly, helped to hold the price down for legitimately graded MS65 or MS65+ pieces. Second, since most collectors collect commemoratives by the 50 piece set, it is much easier and cheaper to find the Grant (no star) in nice mint state condition than the Grant with Star.

The Grant with Star Half Dollar is, in the author's opinion, the sleeping giant of the U.S. silver commemorative series in MS65 or MS65+ condition. In fact, a dealer who owns a strictly graded Superb MS65+ specimen can "name his price" for this coin and the knowledgeable collector will gladly pay it to acquire the coin!

Beware of altered Grants with Star. When a star has been added to the plain Grant, a flat spot, opposite the star's position on the obverse, will appear on the reverse. These fakes are not difficult to detect; however, the collector should always use a 10X magnifying glass when purchasing this issue.

Since most Grants with Star were struck from imperfect dies numerous defects appear on most authentic pieces. Ninety to ninety-five percent of all genuine pieces exhibit the characteristics described below.

The most familiar defect is the rectangular die break between Grant's chin and the G of GRANT. A second diagnostic defect is the pointed clashmark located in front of Grant's tie. Third, on the bridge of Grant's nose is a tiny raised pimple. Fourth, protruding from Grant's head opposite the IT of UNITED is a faint, small, raised square. This is a repair mark on the die. Fifth, there is a clash mark, often mistaken for a die break, extending from A in HALF through the O in DOLLAR. Finally, tilt the coin toward you and a crease will appear in the lower two rays of the star. (Be careful of fake stars which have had a crease engraved in the lower two rays.)

Coins with these characteristics should be genuine. Other genuine varieties without these defects exist. Most of these will exhibit a heavily re-engraved G in GRANT and also the crease in the star. However, because such coins are seldom found it is strongly suggested the collector have the coin authenticated by a responsible authority before purchasing it.

Buying Tips

When purchasing a mint state Grant with Star Half Dollar inspect Grant's cheek and the leaves on the tree for signs of wear.

Of course, MAKE SURE THE COIN IS GENUINE! Pay particular attention to the obverse of the coin because the reverse is usually semi-prooflike and free of problems. An MS65 specimen should be sharply struck. In addition, it should have nice luster, minimum bag marks, and no facial abrasion or slide marks.

An MS65+ piece should exhibit full mint bloom. Also it should be 90% to 100% fully struck and have no detracting marks.

Be sure to examine Grant's features carefully and do not confuse a weak strike for wear. Also be on the lookout for the numerous MS60, AU, and cleaned pieces which are often offered as "Gem BU" or "Superb BU" to the unwary purchaser. Hundreds of dollars can be lost by purchasing an overgraded Grant with Star Half Dollar.

Hawaiian Sesquicentennial
Half Dollar

Net Mintage
9,958

Mint State Frequency
MS60 : 80%
MS65 : 10%
MS65+: 10%

MS65 Retail Price Analysis
1970: $ 485.00
1979: 1,775.00
Appreciation: 266%

Typical Mint State Specimen
MS60: Abrasion, excessive handling marks, poor luster, general poor preservation.

Comments
The 1928 Hawaiian Half Dollar is one of the scarcest commemoratives in Gem MS65 condition. In Superb MS65+ condition this coin is rare.

Most of this issue have been mishandled by the public and now grade AU. Be on the lookout for coins which have been excessively cleaned to appear BU; these are quite plentiful on the market and are often offered at very low prices (20% to 30% lower than wholesale ask levels!) in order to attract the unwary bargain hunters.

The majority of mint state coins usually have one or more problems. Abrasion on Captain Cook's cheekbone on the obverse or on the warrior on the reverse, poor luster, and severe handling marks detract greatly from the coin's appearance. Mint state specimens with these problems should not be graded MS65 or MS65+, but MS60. MS60 specimens should sell for no more than 60% to 70% of MS65 prices.

An MS65 coin will have minimum marks, full luster, a nice strike and no abrasion. An MS65+ piece will be virtually flawless and, while difficult to find, can be purchased with some patience and persistence on the collector's part for a surprisingly modest 10% to 20% premium over an MS65 price. As the years pass by, expect the price premium to dramatically increase for gem pieces.

There is a reported hoard of Hawaiian Half Dollars held by a prominent Hawaiian family estimated to be between 10% to 15% of the entire mintage! Unless the whole hoard is dispersed on the market at once, it should have no adverse effect on this issue's price in the future.

Buying Tips
When purchasing a mint state Hawaiian Half Dollar inspect Captain Cook's cheekbone and the warrior's left hand for signs of wear.

Examine Captain Cook and the warrior for abrasion and slide marks. In addition, look for severe handling marks. Mint state coins with these problems will grade only MS60.

Beware of coins which have been excessively cleaned and retoned to appear BU. They are prevalent on the market today and should not be purchased at uncirculated prices.

An MS65 specimen will exhibit nice luster, minimum marks, a sharp strike, and no slide marks or abrasion.

Be careful of prooflike Hawaiians because counterfeits exist. When buying a prooflike, know your dealer and have the coin authenticated by a reliable authority.

Fifty sandblast proofs were issued. This coin is very rare and should be an excellent long term investment. Such a specimen only appears on the market about once every three or four years and it is much rarer than many other more publicized rarities, such as the 1879 Flowing Hair $4 Gold Piece which sells for well over $15,000 and frequently appears on the market.

Hudson, New York, Sesquicentennial
Half Dollar

Net Mintage
  10,008

Mint State Frequency
  MS60 :   75%
  MS65 :   15%
  MS65+:   10%

MS65 Retail Price Analysis
  1970: $250.00
  1979:   595.00
  Appreciation: 138%

Typical Mint State Specimen
  MS60: Poorly struck, numerous bag marks, abrasion, poor luster.

Comments

The 1935 Hudson Half Dollar is one of the more difficult commemorative half dollars to obtain in Gem MS65 condition. It is extremely difficult to find in Superb MS65+ condition.

A great majority of the low mintage Hudson remain in mint state condition. Original rolls exist. However, because of numerous problems most of them cannot be graded MS65 or MS65+. Most Hudsons were poorly struck, particularly on the reverse on the motto and on Neptune's face and leg. In addition, numerous and severe bag marks can be found on the whale and Neptune, and on the ship's sails. Abrasion is usually prevalent on the center of the lower sail on the ship, the Half Moon. On top of all these problems the coin usually has poor luster; very few Hudsons are found with pleasing iridescent toning. Mint state Hudsons in this condition will grade only MS60 and not MS65 or MS65+. Needless to say, an MS60 Hudson is not a very attractive coin and for this reason will usually sell at least 20% to 25% below an MS65 price.

An MS65 specimen will have a better than average strike, minimum bag marks, and nice luster. In addition, the coin should have only barely noticeable abrasion on the lower sail of the Half Moon.

An MS65+ Hudson should be sharply struck. In addition it should have full mint bloom and no detracting bag marks or abrasion. While a superb Hudson will prove to be extremely difficult to locate, it can be purchased now for a surprisingly small premium of 15% to 20% over a gem price. As the years pass, expect this now modest price differential between MS65 and MS65+ Hudsons to dramatically escalate.

Buying Tips

When purchasing a mint state Hudson Half Dollar inspect the lower sail of the ship and the top of the motto at the word PRETIUM for signs of wear. Make sure an MS65 specimen has a better than average strike, minimum bag marks, nice luster, no slide marks, and just a hint of noticeable abrasion on the center of the lower sail of the ship.

An MS65+ specimen will have a sharp strike (it may be almost impossible to find a full strike), full mint bloom, and no abrasion on the ship's sail. In addition, the coin should not have any detracting bag marks or slide marks.

Beware of coins which have been excessively cleaned to appear BU. They are prevalent on the market and can be easily spotted by the very unnatural brilliance and numerous hairlines on the coin's surfaces.

Huguenot-Walloon Tercentenary
Half Dollar

Net Mintage
142,080

Mint State Frequency
MS60 : 50%
MS65 : 40%
MS65+: 10%

MS65 Retail Price Analysis
1970: $ 26.00
1979: 100.00
Appreciation: 285%

Typical Mint State Specimen
MS60: Poor luster, excessive bag marks.

Comments

The 1924 Huguenot-Walloon Half Dollar is not too difficult to locate in Gem MS65 condition. In Superb MS65+ condition it is moderately difficult to find. About 50% of all mint state specimens will grade MS65 or MS65+.

A great many of this issue were placed into circulation and show some signs of wear. These coins usually grade XF/AU.

Many mint state coins have excessive bag marks on the faces of Coligny and William the Silent on the obverse and on the exposed fields on the reverse. In addition, many also exhibit poor, sometimes dull, luster. Coins with these characteristics cannot grade MS65 or MS65+, but MS60.

An MS65 piece will exhibit nice luster and minimum bag marks. An MS65+ specimen will be virtually flawless and have full mint bloom. A gem can now be purchased for a modest 10% to 15% premium. In the future this premuim will probably be greater as more and more collectors become increasingly quality conscious.

Beware of circulated coins which have been excessively cleaned and are offered as BU. These will display wear and have a very unnatural appearance.

On the reverse of many uncirculated Huguenot-Walloon Half Dollars is a die polishing mark. This mark, which looks like an erasure rub, is located at 11 o'clock at the letters "OT" of HUGUENOT. Since this mark was part of the minting process the coin's grade will not be affected. Many sales have been voided by purchasers who thought this mark was a defect.

Buying Tips

When purchasing a mint state Huguenot-Walloon Half Dollar inspect Governor Coligny's cheek and the ship's stern and crows nest on the center of the main mast for signs of wear.

Make sure an MS65 specimen has nice luster, minimum bag marks, and no slide marks. Be sure the coin has full luster and is not dull in appearance.

An MS65+ specimen will exhibit full mint bloom and be virtually flawless.

Avoid pieces which have been excessively cleaned. They will show rubbing and hairlines and have an unnatural color.

Iowa Centennial
Half Dollar

Net Mintage
100,057

Mint State Frequency
MS60 : 25%
MS65 : 50%
MS65+ : 25%

MS65 Retail Price Analysis
1970: $24.00
1979: 51.00
Appreciation: 113%

Typical Mint State Specimen
MS65: Sharply struck, minimum bag marks, full mint bloom.

Comments
The 1946 Iowa Half Dollar is one of the most common commemorative half dollars in Gem MS65 condition. It is readily available in Superb MS65+ condition.

Most of this issue remain in mint state condition and the great majority of these coins will grade MS65 or MS65+. The two problems which sometimes confront the purchaser of an Iowa are excessive bag marks and a poor strike. A mint state specimen with these problems should be graded MS60.

An MS65 specimen will have minimum bag marks and full mint bloom. In addition, it should be well struck. The eagle's neck will usually exhibit some weakness of strike; however, the coin should still grade MS65 provided the bag marks are at a minimum and it has full mint bloom.

An MS65+ Iowa should be fully struck and have full mint bloom and no detracting marks. For a very small premium of 5% to 10% a superb piece can be purchased today. In the future, this grade coin should be in the greatest demand by quality conscious collectors.

Buying Tips
When purchasing a mint state Iowa Half Dollar inspect the eagle's head and neck and the capitol building for signs of wear.

Make sure an MS65 specimen exhibits minimum bag marks and full mint bloom. Also, the coin should be well struck.

Avoid coins which have been excessively cleaned; these pieces exhibit an unnatural brilliance and many hairlines.

Lexington - Concord Sesquicentennial
Half Dollar

Net Mintage
162,013

Mint State Frequency
MS60 : 50%
MS65 : 40%
MS65+: 10%

MS65 Retail Price Analysis
1970: $15.00
1979: 60.00
Appreciation: 300%

Typical Mint State Specimen
MS60: Weakly struck, abrasion, poor luster, detracting marks.

Comments

The 1925 Lexington-Concord Half Dollar is not too difficult to locate in Gem MS65 condition. In Superb MS65+ condition it is moderately difficult to find. About one-half of all mint state specimens will grade MS65 or MS65+.

A large number of coins have been mishandled or have circulated; most of these pieces will grade XF/AU.

Many of this issue were weakly struck, particularly on the Minute Man's features and gun barrel. Numerous mint state coins display heavy abrasion from having been in the original wooden box of issue. In addition, handling marks, sometimes heavy, also mar this coin's appearance. Furthermore, numerous specimens which remain in the original issue box have an unattractive, heavy green, "mold-like" toning. Mint state pieces which have these problems cannot grade MS65 or MS65+, but MS60.

While MS65 specimens are not too difficult to locate at the present time, MS65+ pieces will prove to be quite elusive. An MS65+ coin will have a full strike and a spectacular frosty mint bloom. Today a superb piece costs only about 15% to 20% more than a gem piece; purchase of superb specimens should be strongly considered before the premium escalates in future years.

Buying Tips

When purchasing a mint state Lexington-Concord Half Dollar inspect the Minute Man's right knee and the corner of the belfry's main structure for signs of wear.

An MS65 specimen should be sharply struck. Also it should have minimum marks, nice luster and no abrasion or slide marks. Since a supply of coins with natural luster or toning is still available today, avoid coins which have the dull, green toning.

An MS65+ specimen should be virtually flawless and exhibit a full strike and frosty mint bloom.

Beware of coins which have been excessively cleaned and are offered as BU. They will exhibit numerous hairlines, show signs of wear, and be unnaturally brilliant.

Lincoln-Illinois Centennial
Half Dollar

Net Mintage
   100,058

Mint State Frequency
MS60 :	60%
MS65 :	30%
MS65+ :	10%

MS65 Retail Price Analysis
1970:	$26.00
1979:	82.00
Appreciation:	215%

Typical Mint State Specimen
   MS60: Poorly struck, excessive bag marks, abrasion.

Comments

The relatively high mintage 1918 Lincoln-Illinois Half Dollar, one of the most beautiful of all commemorative coins, is not an easy coin to find in either Gem MS65 or Superb MS65+ condition.

A great many of this issue have been mishandled or have circulated; most of these specimens will grade AU.

Many mint state specimens encountered today will only grade MS60 because of obvious problems: a poor strike and abrasion and detracting bag marks on Lincoln's face and the obverse fields of the coin.

An MS65 specimen should have minimum bag marks and no abrasion on Lincoln's face or the obverse fields. On many coins the eagle's breast is not fully defined; however, provided the rest of the piece is nice, this should not detract from the coin's condition.

An MS65+ piece should be fully struck and virtually flawless. It should also exhibit a full, frosty mint bloom. A superb Lincoln is a beautiful coin and at present sells for a 15% to 20% premium. In the future, superb pieces will be in the greatest demand by quality conscious collectors and investors. Purchase is recommended.

Buying Tips

When purchasing a mint state Lincoln-Illinois Half Dollar inspect Lincoln's hair above the ear and the eagle's breast for signs of wear. Examine the coin for excessive bag marks, abrasion, and a poor strike. A mint state coin with these problems should grade MS60.

An MS65 specimen should have minimum bag marks, full luster, and no abrasion.

An MS65+ specimen will exhibit a full strike, frosty mint bloom, and be virtually flawless.

Be on the lookout for coins which have been excessively cleaned and are offered as uncirculated. They are very plentiful on the market and are quite unattractive.

Long Island Tercentenary
Half Dollar

Net Mintage
    81,826

Mint State Frequency
MS60 :	30%
MS65 :	55%
MS65+ :	15%

MS65 Retail Price Analysis
1970:	$18.00
1979:	57.50
Appreciation:	214%

Typical Mint State Specimen
    MS65: Full luster, minimum marks, minute sail abrasion.

Comments

The 1936 Long Island Half Dollar is not a difficult commemorative coin to find in Gem MS65 or Superb MS65+ condition.

Many Long Islands have been mishandled or have seen limited circulation; most of these specimens will grade XF/AU.

The major problem which usually plagues this issue is excessive abrasion on the Dutch settler's face and the lower center sail of the Dutch sailing ship. In addition, excessive handling marks often can be found on the obverse on the two faces. Mint state pieces with these problems should grade MS60.

An MS65 specimen should have minimum marks and no abrasion on the obverse and barely noticeable abrasion on the lower mainsail of the ship on the reverse. (This sail abrasion is similar to the problem encountered on many Hudson Half Dollars.)

An MS65+ specimen should not exhibit any abrasion on the reverse sail of the ship. When found, this grade coin can usually be purchased for a modest 10% to 15% premium; in the future this markup will most likely be higher.

Buying Tips

When purchasing a mint state Long Island Half Dollar inspect the Dutch settler's cheek and the ship's lower center sail for signs of wear.

Examine the face for abrasion and marks and the mainsail of the ship for excessive abrasion. Mint state pieces with these problems should not be graded MS65 or MS65+, but MS60.

An MS65 piece should exhibit full luster, minimum marks, no facial abrasion, and barely noticeable sail abrasion.

An MS65+ piece should be virtually flawless with no sail abrasion.

Be careful of the numerous cleaned pieces which are offered as uncirculated; they will have an unnatural and unsightly appearance.

Lynchburg, Virginia, Sesquicentennial
Half Dollar

Net Mintage
20,013

Mint State Frequency
MS60 : 35%
MS65 : 50%
MS65+: 15%

MS65 Retail Price Analysis
1970: $ 38.00
1979: 124.00
Appreciation: 226%

Typical Mint State Specimen
MS65: Full mint bloom, minimum marks, no abrasion.

Comments
The 1936 Lynchburg Half Dollar, despite a low mintage, is not too difficult to find in Gem MS65 condition. A Superb MS65+ specimen is moderately difficult to locate.

A great majority of this issue remains in mint state condition. However, many of these coins exhibit excessive handling marks on Carter Glass' face on the obverse and on Liberty on the reverse. In addition, abrasion is often prevalent on Glass' face and Liberty's breasts. Mint state coins with these problems will grade MS60.

An MS65 coin should exhibit full luster, minimum marks, and no abrasion. On many coins the reverse is semi-prooflike.

An MS65+ specimen should be virtually flawless and one can now be purchased for a modest 15% to 20% premium. With a little patience and perseverance, the collector should be able to find a superb coin for this small markup. This premium will probably be higher in the future.

Buying Tips
When purchasing a mint state Lynchburg Half Dollar inspect Glass' cheekbone and Liberty's breasts for signs of wear.

Examine the coin for abrasion and excessive marks. Uncirculated coins with these problems should not be graded MS65 or MS65+, but MS60.

An MS65 piece should have minimum marks, full mint bloom, and no abrasion. An MS65+ specimen should be virtually flawless.

Avoid coins which exhibit unnatural brilliance and hairlines because they have been harshly cleaned.

Maine Centennial
Half Dollar

Net Mintage
50,028

Mint State Frequency
MS60 : 65%
MS65 : 30%
MS65+: 5%

MS65 Retail Price Analysis
1970: $ 25.00
1979: 115.00
Appreciation: 360%

Typical Mint State Specimen
MS60: Poorly struck, excessive bag marks, dull luster.

Comments
Despite its rather high mintage, the 1920 Maine Half Dollar is a difficult coin to locate in Gem MS65 condition. In Superb MS65+ condition this coin is very scarce.

A great many Maines have been circulated or abused to some degree; most of these pieces will grade XF/AU. In addition, many have suffered from heavy cleaning over the years. Avoid these pieces which are often offered as uncirculated.

Many mint state specimens were very poorly struck, particularly on the obverse. In addition, many exhibit dull luster and suffer from excessive bag marks. Mint state pieces with these problems should grade MS60.

An MS65 coin should have an above average strike, nice luster, and minimum bag marks. Many Maines exhibit heavy, raised die polishing marks on the reverse between the words LIBERTY and MAINE: these should not affect the coin's grade. Make sure the marks are not hairlines which are caused by improper cleaning.

An MS65+ specimen should have fully struck faces on the obverse, full mint bloom, and no detracting marks. Despite being very scarce, superb examples can sometimes be purchased for a modest 20% to 25% premium. This premium could dramatically escalate in the future when the true scarcity of this grade coin becomes apparent. (A superb Maine is much scarcer than many other commemoratives with smaller mintages. For example, the Albany and Antietam Half Dollars, each with total mintages of about one-third of the Maine Half Dollar, still sell for about 50% more than the Maine in superb condition. The knowledgeable collector and investor should realize that now is the time to search for a superb Maine rather than wait until the price reaches its proper level in the future.)

Buying Tips
When purchasing a mint state Maine Half Dollar inspect the left hands of both men and the ribbon bow at the bottom of the wreath for signs of wear.

Be certain an MS65 specimen has nice luster, minimum bag marks, and is sharply struck.

An MS65+ specimen should be fully struck and have full mint bloom and no detracting marks.

Beware of the numerous cleaned pieces which are abundant on the market. These coins will usually exhibit a very unnatural, chrome-like brilliance.

Maryland Tercentenary
Half Dollar

Net Mintage
  25,015

Mint State Frequency
  MS60   :   55%
  MS65   :   40%
  MS65+:   5%

MS65 Retail Price Analysis
  1970: $ 36.50
  1979:   115.00
  Appreciation: 215%

Typical Mint State Specimen
  MS60: Weakly struck, numerous bag marks, abrasion.

Comments

The 1934 Maryland Half Dollar is a difficult coin to locate in Gem MS65 condition. In Superb MS65+ condition it is very difficult to locate.

The majority of this issue remains in mint state condition. However, because of noticeable impairments many of this issue will grade MS60. There is often excessive abrasion on the face and nose of Cecil Calvert and detracting bag marks on both sides of the coin. Also most Marylands were poorly struck.

An MS65 piece should have an above average strike, minor abrasion on the obverse, and minimum bag marks.

An MS65+ specimen should be sharply struck and should not have any detracting marks; only minute abrasion will be evident on the obverse. The author has never seen a mint state Maryland without abrasion on the obverse.

Buying Tips

When purchasing a mint state Maryland Half Dollar inspect Calvert's nose and small crown and the upper left and right tops of the drapery for signs of wear.

Pay particular attention to the strike, bag marks, and abrasion on the coin. Mint state pieces which were poorly struck and have excessive bag marks and abrasion should not grade MS65 or MS65+, but MS60.

An MS65 specimen should be well struck and have minimum bag marks and only minor abrasion on the obverse.

An MS65+ piece should not have any detracting marks. In addition, it should be sharply struck and will exhibit only a touch of abrasion on the obverse.

Beware of coins which have been excessively cleaned and have retoned; these pieces will have an unnatural, flat color.

Missouri Centennial
Half Dollar

Net Mintage
  2★4 Variety: 5,000
  Plain Variety: 15,428

Mint State Frequency
  MS60   :   85%
  MS65   :   10%
  MS65+ :   5%

MS65 Retail Price Analysis
	2★4	Plain
1970:	$155.00	$150.00
1979:	990.00	990.00
Appreciation:	539%	560%

Typical Mint State Specimen
  MS60: Poor luster, excessive abrasion, general poor preservation.

Comments

The 1921 Missouri Half Dollar (both varieties) is one of the most difficult commemorative half dollars to find in Gem MS65 condition. In Superb MS65+ condition this coin is rare.

Most Missouris have seen limited circulation and now grade XF/AU. An abundance of these coins have been cleaned and are offered as BU; they can usually be spotted by the numerous hairlines and chrome-like appearance which they exhibit. The Missouri is one of the most popular coins to clean and overgrade as BU.

All mint state Missouris have a granular surface; and as a result, most toned specimens are mottled or "splotchy" in appearance. There are very few Missouris left today which still retain their natural, original brilliance; most have subdued luster or the mottled toning.

Most of the very few thousand uncirculated coins which survive today should not be graded MS65 or MS65+. They have been mishandled and will exhibit excessive abrasion on the frontiersman's face on the coin's obverse. In addition, the coins also usually display poor luster. Specimens with these problems should be graded MS60. MS60 prices are worth no more than 50% to 60% of MS65 pieces because they are rather plentiful in comparison and not too attractive.

Most Missouris were weakly struck on the hair and coonskin cap of the frontiersman on the obverse and on the powder horn on the reverse. The 2★4 is usually the better struck of the two varieties. When grading a Missouri one should not be overly concerned with this striking weakness, provided the rest of the coin is nice. However, make sure this weakness is not wear!

An MS65 specimen should exhibit nice luster and no noticeable abrasion on the frontiersman's face.

An MS65+ specimen must have full, unbroken color on the face of the frontiersman; also no abrasion should be evident there. Virtually flawless specimens are rare. Probably no more than 1% of the entire two mintages are left today in this ultimate condition. A truly superb Missouri can command a premium of 30% to 50% over a gem price. However, make sure the coin is superb!

A debate exists about the relative scarcity of the lower mintage 2★4 and the plain variety in MS65 or MS65+ condition. The plain variety was distributed first; the 2★4 was sold later. Most of the plains were probably purchased by both collectors and non-collectors while most of the 2★4's were sold to numismatists who desired both varieties for their collections. As a result, most of the plains were subjected to some form of abuse by non-collectors while more of the 2★4's were preserved properly by numismatists. Therefore, both varieties are about equally scarce in MS65 or MS65+ condition, with the plain variety being just a bit scarcer.

The Missouri Half Dollar presents a good lesson for "mintage buffs"; in the past, people who relied solely on mintages to determine scarcity would pay a 20% to 30% premium for the lower mintage 2★4. Today, however, the prices are equal for either variety.

Buying Tips

When purchasing a mint state Missouri Half Dollar inspect the hair behind the frontiersman's ear and the scout's left shoulder and arm for signs of wear.

An MS65 specimen should not exhibit any slide marks or noticeable facial abrasion. In addition, the piece must have nice, natural luster.

An MS65+ piece should display full, unbroken color on the frontiersman's face and no facial abrasion. Also the coin must possess full mint bloom.

Be certain not to purchase as BU one of the numerous cleaned coins on the market. One can be spotted by its chrome-like appearance and numerous hairlines.

Monroe Doctrine Centennial
Half Dollar

Net Mintage
    274,077

Mint State Frequency
    MS60 :   75%
    MS65 :   20%
    MS65+:   5%

MS65 Retail Price Analysis
    1970: $18.00
    1979:   91.00
    Appreciation: 406%

Typical Mint State Specimen
    MS60: Poorly struck, dull luster, abrasion, numerous bag marks.

Comments

The 1923-S Monroe Half Dollar is quite difficult to locate in Gem MS65 condition and is extremely difficult to find in Superb MS65+ condition.

A vast majority of Monroes have been abused or have circulated over the years. Most of these will grade between VF and AU. Many pieces have been excessively cleaned and are offered as BU. Do not purchase these specimens at uncirculated prices.

Most Monroes were poorly struck, particularly on the hair detail of Adams on the obverse and on North and South America on the reverse. In addition, many mint state pieces exhibit poor luster, abrasion on the obverse, and numerous bag marks, particularly on Adams' face. Mint state coins with these problems should not be graded MS65 or MS65+, but MS60. Needless to say, these coins are very unattractive and should sell for no more than 40% to 50% of MS65 prices.

An MS65 specimen should be well struck. Also, it will have nice luster, minimum bag marks, and no abrasion.

An MS65+ piece must have virtually full facial detail on the two females on the reverse. The author has never seen a Monroe with full, sharp detail on the reverse. In addition, a superb example should be fully lustrous and exhibit no detracting marks. A superb Monroe can be purchased at the present for a premium of about 30% to 40%. They have been known to sell for as high as 100% more. Since they are very difficult to find, this premium could be substantially more in the future.

Buying Tips

When purchasing a mint state Monroe Half Dollar inspect Adams' cheekbone and North America's left arm for signs of wear.

Make sure an MS65 specimen is well struck, and has nice luster and no slide marks or abrasion. Also, the piece should have minimum bag marks.

An MS65+ specimen should exhibit most of the facial detail on North and South America. In addition, it should have full, frosty mint bloom and be virtually flawless.

Beware of the many cleaned pieces on the market today. They will display numerous hairlines and have an unnatural brilliance.

New Rochelle, New York
Half Dollar

Net Mintage
15,266

Mint State Frequency
MS60 : 40%
MS65 : 40%
MS65+: 20%

MS65 Retail Price Analysis
1970: $ 67.50
1979: 245.00
Appreciation: 263%

Typical Mint State Specimen
MS65: Full luster, minimum abrasion and bag marks.

Comments

The 1938 New Rochelle Half Dollar, despite a low mintage, is not too difficult to find in Gem MS65 or Superb MS65+ condition.

The great majority of this issue is still available in mint state condition. All uncirculated specimens will show some abrasion on the middle of the fleur-de-lis on the reverse. However, many of these coins will exhibit excessive abrasion on this area and also on the calf's body on the obverse. In addition, some coins will display numerous bag marks or "tractor marks", from the reeded edges of other coins, on the exposed fields on both the obverse and reverse. Mint state specimens with these problems should not be graded MS65 or MS65+, but MS60.

An MS65 specimen should have minimum abrasion on the fleur-de-lis and no noticeable abrasion on the calf's body. Also the coin must display full luster and have minimum bag marks.

An MS65+ piece should exhibit only minute abrasion on the fleur-de-lis and none on the calf. In addition, it will have full mint bloom and no detracting marks. A virtually flawless gem New Rochelle is not too difficult to find at the present and can sometimes be purchased for a modest 15% to 20% premium. As collectors become increasingly quality conscious expect this premium to be higher in the future.

Buying Tips

When purchasing a mint state New Rochelle Half Dollar inspect the calf's hip and the fleur-de-lis for signs of wear.

Examine the fleur-de-lis and calf for excessive abrasion and slide marks. In addition, look for severe bag or "tractor" marks on the exposed fields on the coin. Mint state specimens with these problems must be graded MS60.

An MS65 piece should display minimum abrasion on the fleur-de-lis and no noticeable abrasion on the calf. Also the coin must have full mint bloom, minimum bag marks, and no slide marks.

An MS65+ specimen should be virtually flawless and will exhibit only a minute amount of friction on the fleur-de-lis.

While both gem and superb pieces will possess full, frosty mint bloom, some coins can be found with prooflike fields for a modest premium of 20% to 25%. Purchase of these specimens is recommended for future price appreciation.

Norfolk, Virginia, Bicentennial
Half Dollar

Net Mintage
16,936

Mint State Frequency
MS60 : 30%
MS65 : 40%
MS65+: 30%

MS65 Retail Price Analysis
1970: $ 57.50
1979: 237.50
Appreciation: 313%

Typical Mint State Specimen
MS65: Minimum marks, full, frosty mint bloom.

Comments
The 1936 Norfolk Half Dollar, despite its low mintage, is readily available today in Gem MS65 or Superb MS65+ condition.

Like the Antietam Half Dollar, the fields of all mint state Norfolks have a brilliant, chiseled, "ripple" effect.

Almost all Norfolks remain in mint state condition and most of these can be graded MS65 or MS65+. However, some uncirculated specimens will exhibit many handling marks on the ship's sails on the obverse and on the fields on the reverse. Mint state pieces with these problems should be graded MS60, not MS65 or MS65+.

An MS65 piece will have full mint bloom and minimum marks.

An MS65+ specimen will be virtually flawless. A Norfolk is one of the easiest low mintage commemoratives to find in this ultimate condition. With a little patience on the collector's part, a superb specimen can usually be found for a modest premium of about 10%. The premium will probably increase a bit in the future.

Buying Tips
When purchasing a mint state Norfolk Half Dollar inspect the sails of the ship and the center of the royal mace for signs of wear.

An MS65 specimen should have minimum marks, full mint bloom, and no slide marks.

An MS65+ piece will be virtually problem free and possess blazing mint bloom.

Be on the lookout for coins which have been excessively cleaned; they will exhibit a very unnatural, dull appearance and are quite unattractive.

Oregon Trail Memorial
Half Dollar

Net Mintage
(Note: The D&S mint marks can be found on the obverse to the left of the Indian's right foot.)

1926 :	47,955	1934D:	7,006	1938 :	6,006	1939 :	3,004
1926S:	83,055	1936 :	10,006	1938D:	6,005	1939D:	3,004
1928 :	6,028	1936S :	5,006	1938S :	6,006	1939S :	3,005
1933D:	5,008	1937D:	12,008				

MS65 Retail Price Analysis

	1926	1926S	1928	1933D	1934D	1936
1970:	$15.00	$15.00	$ 20.00	$ 35.00	$ 16.00	$15.00
1979:	85.00	85.00	215.00	230.00	180.00	92.00
Appreciation:	467%	467%	975%	557%	1025%	513%

	1936S	1937D	1938PDS	1939PDS	Type
1970:	$ 20.00	$15.00	$ 45.00	$125.00	$15.00
1979:	205.00	90.00	420.00	555.00	85.00
Appreciation:	925%	500%	833%	344%	467%

Mint State Frequency (Type Coin Only)
- MS60 : 30%
- MS65 : 50%
- MS65+ : 20%

Typical Mint State Specimen (Type Coin Only)
MS65: Full luster, no detracting marks.

Comments

The Oregon Trail Half Dollar type coin, perhaps the most beautiful U.S. coin ever made and certainly one of the best examples of true Americana, is one of the easiest commemoratives to locate in Gem MS65 or Superb MS65+ condition. To acquire a gem or superb PDS set, however, will require more searching on the collector's part because some PDS sets have only one or two gem coins while the others in the set may not be as nice.

Many uncirculated Oregon Trails have excessive bag marks, particularly prominent on the knee and body of the Indian on the obverse. Mint state coins with these marks should not be graded MS65 or MS65+, but MS60.

An MS65 specimen will have minimum bag marks and full mint bloom.

An MS65+ specimen should be virtually flawless and can usually be purchased for a modest 10% to 15% premium. Purchase of these superb pieces, particularly the very low mintage single mint issues, is strongly recommended because of their beauty, scarcity, and present low prices.

The 1926 and 1926S coins are the two dates usually sold as type coins today and are quite plentiful in gem condition. The 1926S, in addition, can often be found with a very pleasing semi-prooflike, frosty mint bloom.

All 1928 pieces have an unusual rim indentation located at the four o'clock position on the obverse. The coin is sometimes very thick at this position and very thin at the opposite side of the coin. This indentation was probably caused by uneven striking pressure of the dies. Other Oregon Trail issues usually have similar indentation but they are not as pronounced as those on the 1928 issue.

The 1933D and 1934D issues can sometimes be found with a minor triple repunching on the lettering on the obverse. This is particularly noticeable on the letters "ALF" of the HALF.

Some issues of the Oregon Trail were weakly struck on the first "T" of the word STATES on the obverse and on the details of the pioneer leading the oxen and the Conestoga wagon on the reverse. (The 1933D is the best example of this weak striking.) A striking weakness should not be confused with actual wear on the coin.

Since most collectors today collect commemoratives by type, demand for the scarcer singles or the two PDS sets is not great at the moment. When collectors or investors begin to notice the extremely low mintages of these coins, price rises could be spectacular. It may take as long as five or ten years before the prices escalate dramatically, but for the long term investment these coins look like winners; they combine beauty, very low mintages, and, for now, low prices. The 1928, 1933D, 1934D, and 1936S with mintages between 5,006 and 7,006, should be the best bets for long term investment. The 1936 and 1937D, with mintages of 10,006 and 12,008, should also perform well in the future. The 1939 PDS set should sell for much more than the 1938 PDS set. Its mintage is approximately one-half of the 1938 set's mintage.

Buying Tips

When purchasing a mint state Oregon Trail Half Dollar inspect the Indian's knee and the ox's hip for signs of wear.

Make sure an MS65 or MS65+ specimen has full, frosty mint bloom and minimum bag marks.

When buying the PDS sets examine each coin exactly as you would a type coin. If one or more of the three coins does not meet MS65 standards do not purchase the set at MS65 prices. A PDS set's price and demand are lowered a great deal by the condition of the worst coin.

Beware of cleaned pieces — they will be very unnatural in appearance and are quite unattractive.

Panama-Pacific Exposition
Half Dollar

Net Mintage
27,134

Mint State Frequency
MS60 : 90%
MS65 : 8%
MS65+: 2%

MS65 Retail Price Analysis
1970: $ 85.00
1979:   980.00
Appreciation: 1,053%

Typical Mint State Specimen
MS60: Poorly struck, abrasion, excessive handling marks, possible light cleaning.

Comments

The 1915-S Panama-Pacific Half Dollar is one of the most difficult commemoratives to locate in Gem MS65 condition. In Superb MS65+ condition it is almost impossible to find.

Most of this issue have seen circulation or have been abused because of mishandling or excessive cleaning. In fact, the "Pan-Pac" is one of the greatest victims of cleaning in the entire commemorative series.

The vast majority of the few thousand mint state Pan-Pacs which survive today cannot be graded MS65 or MS65+ because of numerous problems: abrasion on Columbia's left arm and shoulder and weak strike on the eagle's neck and breast. Also many handling marks, particularly on Columbia on the obverse and the shield on the reverse, plague this issue. Uncirculated coins with these problems will grade MS60.

Furthermore, be careful of pieces which were harshly cleaned many years ago and have naturally retoned with a beautiful iridescence. To the inexperienced collector, these pieces appear to be exceptional in quality. However, upon careful inspection the collector will often discover hairlines and rubbing on the high points. The author does not wish to imply all toned Pan-Pacs are toned AU's but only that the novice should take extra care before purchasing such a coin.

Some specimens exhibit reengraved breast feathers on the eagle. Be alert and study both sides of the coin before purchasing it. Rubbing will be apparent on the obverse of a coin which has reengraved breast feathers. Reengraving is another method unscrupulous sellers use to enhance a coin. Do not be fooled by this practice; know how to tell the difference between AU and uncirculated coins!

All pieces seen by the author have a circular depression running completely around the obverse and reverse perimeters of each coin. This depression ranges from light to heavy in appearance. In addition, the majority of Pan-Pacs have a planchet flaw over the "D" in Dollar on the reverse and to the right of Columbia's cap on the obverse. The rim looks "pinched" at this spot; it is similar to the rim indentation which is so prominent on the 1928 Oregon Trail. This flaw should not detract from the overall value of the coin.

An MS65 piece should be sharply struck and have no noticeable abrasion; in addition, it should have minimum marks and full mint bloom.

An MS65+ specimen will have a beautiful satiny luster and should be fully struck. In addition, it should not have any detracting marks or abrasion. A superb specimen is spectacular in appearance and should command a substantial premium of 50% to 75% more than a gem piece. It may take months, or even years, of searching to locate a truly superb specimen.

Buying Tips

When purchasing a mint state Panama-Pacific Half Dollar inspect Liberty's shoulder and the eagle's breast for signs of wear.

Together with the Isabella, Lafayette, Alabama, Grant with Star, Missouri, and a few other issues, the Pan-Pac is one of the most frequently overgraded commemorative issues. Gem or superb pieces are very difficult to find so do not expect to find one and pay the wholesale "Bid" for it! Remember, you get what you pay for.

Pay particular attention to the strike of the coin. An MS65 specimen should be sharply struck and have full mint bloom and minimum marks. In addition, it should not exhibit any abrasion or slide marks.

An MS65+ piece will exhibit a satiny, full mint bloom. Furthermore, it should be fully struck and virtually flawless.

Avoid the many cleaned pieces which are advertised on the market today as BU. They will be very unattractive and exhibit numerous hairlines and rubbing. Be very careful when buying a toned piece because the toning may be hiding one or more of the numerous problems often encountered with this issue.

Pilgrim Tercentenary
Half Dollar

Net Mintage
  1920: 152,112
  1921: 20,053

MS65 Retail Price Analysis

	1920	1921
1970:	$18.00	$ 66.00
1979:	57.50	125.50
Appreciation:	219%	92%

Mint State Frequency (Type Coin Only)
  MS60 : 45%
  MS65 : 45%
  MS65+: 10%

Typical Mint State Specimen (Type Coin Only)
  MS65: Sharply struck, minimum bag marks, full luster.

Comments

The 1920 and 1921 Pilgrim Half Dollars are two of the easier commemoratives to purchase in Gem MS65 condition. However, they are not as easy to find in Superb MS65+ condition as is generally believed.

Many of the Pilgrims, particularly the large mintage 1920 issue, have seen circulation; most of these will grade XF/AU. In addition, some of this issue have been heavily cleaned and are being offered as BU. These specimens will display numerous hairlines and exhibit wear.

Many Pilgrims were poorly struck on the reverse on the ship's mast and its other very detailed areas. In addition, some specimens exhibit numerous bag marks, which are particularly evident on the coin's obverse. Mint state coins with these problems cannot be graded MS65 or MS65+, but MS60.

An MS65 piece will have a sharp strike, minimum bag marks, and full luster.

An MS65+ specimen, which should be virtually flawless, can sometimes be purchased at the present for a modest 10% to 20% premium. This markup will probably increase in the future when collectors become more quality conscious.

The 1921 issue has an interesting die variety. On the obverse on the fields of the coin can be found numerous raised lines and "bumps". On the reverse, near the stern of the ship, are several obverse letters from IN GOD WE TRUST. This variety is a result of badly clashed dies. (Die clashing occurs when the obverse and reverse dies come together without a planchet in place. The result is some details from the obverse die become struck onto the reverse die and vice versa.) The lines on the obverse are polishing marks. The raised "bumps" on the obverse match up with the detail on the reverse.

This variety breaks up the already low 1921 mintage of 20,053 into two smaller groups, for which, at the present, no premium is charged. In fact, many collectors mistake a coin which has the die clashing characteristics for a piece which has been cleaned or abused. Know the difference before purchasing the coin.

Buying Tips

When purchasing a mint state Pilgrim Half Dollar inspect the pilgrim's hair and the ship's stern for signs of wear.

Be certain an MS65 or MS65+ specimen has full mint bloom, minimum bag marks, and a sharp strike. In addition, make sure the coin has not been badly cleaned. (On the variety, the fields will have raised lines while on a cleaned piece the lines will be tiny scratches.)

The 1920 issue is a favorite of the "cleaning merchant": XF or AU pieces are harshly cleaned in a poor attempt to simulate original luster and are often offered as BU for 20% to 50% below the wholesale bid price! Remember, there are very few bargains in numismatics — you get what you pay for.

Rhode Island (Providence) Tercentenary
Half Dollar

Net Mintage
(Note: The D & S mint marks can be found on the obverse to the left of the Indian's right foot.)
  1936 :   20,013
  1936D: 15,010
  1936S :   15,011

Mint State Frequency (Type Coin Only)
  MS60   :   35%
  MS65   :   45%
  MS65+:   20%

MS65 Retail Price Analysis

	1936PDS	Type
1970:	$ 52.00	$17.50
1979:	260.00	85.00
Appreciation:	400%	386%

Typical Mint State Specimen
(Type Coin Only)
MS65: Full luster, minimum bag marks, no abrasion.

Comments

The Rhode Island Half Dollar, which looks more like a medal than a coin, is one of the easiest type coins to locate in Gem MS65 condition. It is not too difficult to find in Superb MS65+ condition.

The Rhode Island PDS sets are easier to acquire in MS65 condition than most other commemorative PDS issues. However, before buying an entire set at MS65 prices, be certain that each coin in the set grades MS65!

Most of this issue is available in mint state condition today. However, many coins will exhibit abrasion on Roger Williams and the Indian on the obverse and on the anchor on the reverse. In addition, excessive bag marks also trouble this issue. Mint state coins with these problems should not be graded MS65 or MS65+, but MS60.

An MS65 piece will have nice luster, minimum bag marks, and no abrasion.

An MS65+ specimen should be virtually flawless and can be purchased at the present for a small 10% to 15% premium. This grade coin will be in the greatest demand in the future by collectors and investors.

Buying Tips

When purchasing a mint state Rhode Island Half Dollar inspect the Indian's shoulder and the middle of the anchor for signs of wear.

An MS65 or MS65+ specimen should exhibit full mint bloom, minimum bag marks, and no abrasion or slide marks.

When buying a PDS set examine each coin exactly as you would a type coin. If one of the three coins does not meet MS65 standards do not purchase the set at MS65 prices. A PDS set's demand and price are lowered greatly by the condition of the worst coin.

Beware of cleaned pieces; they will exhibit many hairlines and will look unnaturally polished.

Roanoke Island, North Carolina
Half Dollar

Net Mintage
29,030

Mint State Frequency
MS60 : 35%
MS65 : 45%
MS65+: 20%

MS65 Retail Price Analysis
1970: $28.00
1979: 99.00
Appreciation: 254%

Typical Mint State Specimen
MS65: Full mint bloom, minimum marks.

Comments
The 1937 Roanoke Half Dollar is not a difficult coin to find in Gem MS65 or Superb MS65+ condition at the present time.

Most Roanokes remain in mint state conditon. Uncirculated coins which exhibit numerous handling marks, particularly on Sir Walter Raleigh's face and hat brim on the obverse and on Eleanor Dare on the reverse, should be graded MS60.

An MS65 specimen will have minimum marks and full mint bloom.

An MS65+ piece should be virtually flawless and will exhibit a nice frosty mint bloom. At the present, a superb specimen can be purchased for a modest 10% to 15% premium and should be strongly considered by the collector because premium quality coins will be in the greatest demand in the future.

Buying Tips
When purchasing a mint state Roanoke Half Dollar inspect the brim of the hat and Eleanor Dare's left arm and the front of her dress for signs of wear.

Make sure an MS65 or MS65+ specimen has full mint bloom and no detracting marks. Some pieces can be found frosty and semi-prooflike for a modest premium. Purchase of these coins is recommended.

Avoid the many cleaned pieces which are offered as BU to the unwary purchaser. They will exhibit many hairlines and will have an unnatural, polished appearance.

Robinson-Arkansas Centennial
Half Dollar

Net Mintage
25,265

Mint State Frequency
MS60 : 50%
MS65 : 40%
MS65+ : 10%

MS65 Retail Price Analysis
1970: $24.00
1979: 86.00
Appreciation: 258%

Typical Mint State Specimen
MS60: Excessive bag marks, abrasion.

Comments
The Robinson-Arkansas Half Dollar is a more difficult coin to locate in Gem MS65 or Superb MS65+ condition than is generally believed.

The majority of this issue remains in mint state condition. Many, however, will grade MS60 because of obvious impairments: excessive abrasion and numerous bag marks, particularly on the face of Senator Robinson. Coins with these problems should not be graded MS65 or MS65+.

An MS65 coin will have nice luster, minimum bag marks, and no abrasion. Some pieces also exhibit a striking weakness on Robinson's hair but this characteristic should not detract from the coin's grade, provided the rest of the coin is nice. (Make sure the weakness is not rubbing caused from circulation.)

An MS65+ specimen should be virtually flawless and sharply struck. A superb example can now be purchased for a small premium of 10% to 15%. This is a small markup to pay to guarantee the coin's resaleability in the future.

Buying Tips
When purchasing a mint state Robinson-Arkansas Half Dollar inspect Robinson's cheek and the top of the eagle's left wing and head for signs of wear.

An MS65 specimen should have minimum bag marks, full mint bloom, and no slide marks or abrasion.

An MS65+ piece will be sharply struck and virtually flawless.

San Diego, California-Pacific Exposition
Half Dollar

Net Mintage
(Note: The D & S mint marks can be found on the reverse below the motto).

1935S:	70,132
1936D:	30,092

Mint State Frequency

MS60	:	35%
MS65	:	50%
MS65+	:	15%

MS65 Retail Price Analysis

	1935S	1936D
1970:	$17.00	$19.00
1979:	55.00	98.00
Appreciation:	224%	416%

Typical Mint State Specimen
MS65: Full luster, minimum bag marks, sharply struck, no abrasion.

Comments

The San Diego Half Dollar (both years) is one of the easiest commemorative coins to locate in Gem MS65 condition. It is not too difficult to find in Superb MS65+ condition.

Most 1935-S and 1936-D San Diegos remain in mint state condition. However, many were poorly struck; others have abrasion across Minerva's legs on the obverse. To a lesser degree, excessive bag marks are another problem encountered with this issue. Uncirculated specimens with these problems should be graded MS60.

An MS65 coin will be sharply struck and have minimum bag marks. In addition, the piece should have full luster and no abrasion.

An MS65+ coin should be fully struck, frosty, and virtually defect free. A superb specimen can sometimes be purchased for a very modest 5% to 10% premium. In this condition the coin is very beautiful and the premium should increase in the future.

Many San Diegos exhibit a weak strike on the vertical lines on Minerva's breastplate. In addition, weakness often appears on her helmet and the California Tower on the reverse. The 1936-D is usually a better struck coin than the 1935-S. On occasion, the 1935-S is so poorly struck the S mint mark looks like a rectangular blur. In MS65+, fully struck condition the 1935-S is more difficult to find than the lower mintage 1936-D.

Buying Tips

When purchasing a mint state San Diego Half Dollar inspect Minerva's knees and the top right side of the tower for signs of wear.

An MS65 specimen should have minimum bag marks and no slide marks or abrasion. In addition, the piece should be sharply struck and have full luster.

An MS65+ specimen should be fully struck and virtually problem free; it will also have a pleasing frosty mint bloom.

Sesquicentennial Of American Independence
Half Dollar

Net Mintage
141,120

Mint State Frequency
MS60 : 90%
MS65 : 10%
MS65+ : --%

MS65 Retail Price Analysis
1970: $17.50
1979: 57.00
Appreciation: 226%

Typical Mint State Specimen
MS60: Poorly struck, excessive abrasion, severe bag marks, poor luster and color.

Comments
The 1926 Sesquicentennial Half Dollar is a very difficult coin to locate in Gem MS65 condition. In the author's opinion this coin probably does not exist in true Superb MS65+ condition.

This issue was struck in very low relief and thus much detail has been lost on the obverse and reverse. (The inscription on the Liberty Bell is almost impossible to read.) Thousands of these coins circulated and most grade between VF and AU.

Almost all mint state coins were poorly struck and exhibit an overabundance of abrasion and "pockmarks" on Washington's cheek. In addition, many "Sesquis" have poor color and dull luster. Severe bag marks also plague this issue. To say coins with these characteristics are unattractive is an understatement. In fact, this issue looks as if it were struck at the mint in AU condition!

An MS65 specimen should exhibit an above average strike, minimum abrasion and bag marks, and nice luster and color. The author has never seen a Sesqui with a perfect cheek on the face.

Almost all Sesquis' luster looks unnatural, but cleaned coins look absolutely awful — the cleaning just accentuates all the coin's defects.

As an investment, the author suggests the collector or investor look elsewhere; buy one coin for your set, forget about it, and concentrate on the many other issues which have such tremendous potential.

Buying Tips
When purchasing a mint state Sesquicentennial Half Dollar inspect the upper third of the Liberty Bell for signs of wear. Because of the excessive abrasion and marks typically found on Washington's cheekbone it is very difficult to differentiate wear on an AU coin from the normal facial abrasion found on an MS60 specimen. In effect, an MS60 piece often looks like an AU specimen.

Make sure an MS65 specimen has nice luster and color, a better than average strike, minimum bag marks, and only a small amount of abrasion on Washington's cheek.

In true MS65+ condition this coin probably does not exist. The author has seen many specimens which have been buffed to remove the abrasion on Washington's face. However, the buffing leaves numerous hairlines on the coin and accentuates its other problems.

Old Spanish Trail
Half Dollar

Net Mintage
 10,008

Mint State Frequency
 MS60 : 40%
 MS65 : 40%
 MS65+: 20%

MS65 Retail Price Analysis
 1970: $235.00
 1979: 525.00
 Appreciation: 123%

Typical Mint State Specimen
 MS65: Full luster, no abrasion, minimum marks.

Comments
The 1935 Spanish Trail Half Dollar, one of the best designed commemoratives, is a moderately scarce coin to find in Gem MS65 condition. In Superb MS65+ condition it is difficult to locate but can be found with some perseverance on the collector's part.

Not too many Spanish Trails saw circulation, but many have been abused or excessively cleaned. Avoid these coins which are being offered as BU. They will have numerous hairlines and an unnatural brilliance.

Many mint state pieces exhibit excessive, and sometimes severe, handling marks on the steer's head and on the exposed fields on the obverse and reverse. (Some specimens exhibit light, raised die polishing marks in the fields, but these should not detract from the coin's overall grade.) In addition, the steer's head can often be found with abrasion on it. Mint state specimens with these problems should not be graded MS65 or MS65+, but MS60.

An MS65 coin will have full luster, minimum marks, and no abrasion.

An MS65+ specimen, which should be virtually flawless, can usually be purchased for a 10% to 15% premium over an MS65 price. This markup will probably increase in the future when collectors become more and more quality conscious.

As an investment this coin has both beauty of design and low mintage in its favor.

Buying Tips
When purchasing a mint state Spanish Trail Half Dollar inspect the steer's head and the middle of the yucca tree for signs of wear.

To grade MS65 the coin must not have any slide marks or abrasion on the steer's head. It should also have minimum marks and full mint bloom.

An MS65+ specimen, with no detracting marks and full mint bloom, should be problem free. In superb, virtually flawless condition the Spanish Trail Half Dollar is the easiest key coin to locate in the fifty piece type set.

Do not purchase at BU prices the many cleaned pieces on the market; they can be spotted by the abundant hairlines and unnatural color on the surfaces.

Stone Mountain Memorial
Half Dollar

Net Mintage
   1,314,709

Mint State Frequency
MS60 :	25%
MS65 :	55%
MS65+ :	20%

MS65 Retail Price Analysis
1970:	$12.00
1979:	33.50
Appreciation:	179%

Typical Mint State Specimen
   MS65: Sharply struck, minimum bag marks, full mint bloom.

Comments

The 1925 Stone Mountain Half Dollar is one of the easiest commemoratives to find in Gem MS65 condition. In Superb MS65+ condition this type is not difficult to locate.

A majority of Stone Mountains have circulated and most can grade anywhere between Fine and AU. Many specimens are cleaned and offered as BU by unscrupulous sellers for ridiculously low prices (anywhere between 50% to 70% of wholesale bid!) These cleaned pieces will exhibit hairlines and wear and look polished.

Most specimens which remain in uncirculated condition can be graded MS65 or MS65+. However, some were poorly struck on General Lee's leg on the obverse and on the eagle's breast on the reverse and others exhibit many bag marks. Mint state coins with these problems should be graded MS60.

An MS65 piece will be sharply struck and have full mint bloom and minimum marks.

An MS65+ specimen should be fully struck and virtually flawless. Also it will have a beautiful "powdery" satin surface. At the present these coins can be purchased for a modest 10% to 20% premium. In the future this premium could easily increase.

Buying Tips

When purchasing a mint state Stone Mountain Half Dollar inspect Lee's left elbow and the eagle's breast for signs of wear.

An MS65 specimen should be sharply struck. In addition, it should have full mint bloom and minimum marks.

An MS65+ piece will be fully struck and exhibit a very attractive powdery, satin mint bloom.

Beware of the numerous cleaned pieces advertised as BU for ridiculously low prices; these polished specimens can be spotted by the many hairlines and rubbing spots on the coins.

Texas Independence Centennial
Half Dollar

Net Mintage
(Note: The D&S mint marks can be found on the reverse under Victory's left knee and above the "T" in the word THE.)

1934 :	61,463						
1935 :	9,996	1936 :	8,911	1937 :	6,571	1938 :	3,780
1935D:	10,007	1936D:	9,039	1937D:	6,605	1938D:	3,775
1935S :	10,008	1936S :	9,055	1937S :	6,637	1938S :	3,814

MS65 Retail Price Analysis

	1934	1935PDS	1936PDS	1937PDS	1938PDS	Type
1970:	$19.00	$ 50.00	$ 50.00	$ 55.00	$110.00	$17.00
1979:	51.00	175.00	172.50	235.00	515.00	54.00
Appreciation:	168%	250%	245%	327%	368%	218%

Mint State Frequency (Type Coin Only)
- MS60 : 30%
- MS65 : 45%
- MS65+: 25%

Typical Mint State Specimen (Type Coin Only)
MS65: Full luster, minimum marks, no noticeable abrasion.

Comments

The Texas Half Dollar is one of the easiest commemorative type coins to find in Gem MS65 or Superb MS65+ condition. To acquire a gem or superb PDS set will require more searching on the collector's part because many PDS sets often have only one or two gem coins while the other coins in the set are not as nice. However, the Texas sets are easier to locate in nice condition than most of the other issues' PDS sets.

Very few Texas pieces circulated. Some mint state specimens display deep handling marks, particularly on the obverse on the eagle. In addition, excessive abrasion can sometimes be found on Victory's right knee. Uncirculated coins with these problems should be graded MS60, and not MS65 or MS65+.

An MS65 specimen should have minimum marks, full luster, and no noticeable abrasion on Victory's right knee.

An MS65+ coin will be virtually flawless and should not exhibit any abrasion on the knee.

The 1934 issue, with a mintage of over 60,000, is the most common of all the Texas issues.

Since most commemorative collectors do not collect the complete 144 piece set, demand for PDS sets, in general, is not great. The Texas sets are no exception to this rule. The 1935, 1936, and 1937 sets are not too difficult to find. The 1938 PDS set, with a set mintage under 3,800, is the scarcest of the four sets. Many mint state 1938 P, D, and S coins exhibit a chrome-like luster. This is not unusual and should not affect the coin's grade. However, be certain the coin has not been cleaned.

Buying Tips

When purchasing a mint state Texas Half Dollar inspect the eagle's breast and Liberty's head and knee for signs of wear.

An MS65 specimen should have minimum marks and no noticeable abrasion should be evident on Victory's right knee. Most S mint pieces were struck with flat knees. The collector should not be overly concerned with this characteristic provided the rest of the coin is nice.

An MS65+ piece will be virtually flawless and should not exhibit any knee friction.

When buying the PDS sets examine each coin exactly as you would a type coin. If one of the three pieces does not meet the standards for MS65 do not purchase the set at MS65 prices. A PDS set's demand and price are lowered greatly by the condition of the worst coin.

Fort Vancouver Centennial
Half Dollar

Net Mintage
14,994

Mint State Frequency
MS60 : 60%
MS65 : 35%
MS65+: 5%

MS65 Retail Price Analysis
1970: $ 92.50
1979: 435.00
Appreciation: 370%

Typical Mint State Specimen
MS60: Poorly struck, abrasion, excessive handling marks.

Comments
The 1925 Fort Vancouver Half Dollar is a scarce coin in MS65 condition. In Superb MS65+ condition it is very scarce.

Many Fort Vancouvers have been mishandled and most of these will grade AU. Others have been harshly cleaned and are being offered as BU; these can be spotted by the many hairlines and general polished appearance on the surfaces.

Many specimens were poorly struck, particularly on McLaughlin's hair and the frontiersman's strap and left shin. In addition, the majority of mint state pieces exhibit abrasion on McLaughlin's left shoulder and many handling marks on his face and the obverse fields of the coin. Uncirculated coins with these problems should be graded MS60.

An MS65 specimen should be sharply struck and have full mint bloom and minimum marks. Also it should not exhibit any abrasion. Most pieces display some flatness on the frontiersman's left shin. Minor flatness in this area is tolerable for an MS65 coin provided the rest of the coin is choice.

An MS65+ specimen, which should be virtually flawless, will be fully struck and exhibit a full, frosty mint bloom. Superb pieces are very scarce today, but when one is found it can sometimes be purchased for a rather modest 20% to 25% premium. This markup should prove to be a bargain in the future.

Some pieces exhibit semi-prooflike luster. A gem or superb specimen with this luster would be a real find for the enterprising numismatist!

Most coins seen by the author exhibit tiny "bubbles", caused by die chips, on the reverse above the mountain on the right.

Buying Tips
When purchasing a mint state Fort Vancouver Half Dollar inspect McLaughlin's temple and the frontiersman's right knee for signs of wear.

An MS65 specimen should be sharply struck and have full mint bloom, minimum marks, and no slide marks or abrasion.

An MS65+ piece should be fully struck and virtually flawless. In addition, it will exhibit a full, frosty mint bloom.

Beware of the many cleaned pieces on the market; they will exhibit numerous hairlines and look polished.

Vermont Sesquicentennial
Half Dollar

Net Mintage
28,142

Mint State Frequency
MS60 :   50%
MS65 :   40%
MS65+:   10%

MS65 Retail Price Analysis
1970: $ 38.00
1979:   137.50
Appreciation: 262%

Typical Mint State Specimen
MS60: Severe handling marks, excessive abrasion.

Comments

The 1927 Vermont Half Dollar, which was struck in high relief, is not as easy to find in Gem MS65 condition as many collectors believe. In Superb MS65+ condition this issue is quite scarce.

Most Vermonts remain in mint state condition. However, many specimens exhibit excessive abrasion on Ira Allen's cheek and the catamount's flank and severe handling marks, particularly on Allen's face. Uncirculated coins with these problems should not be graded MS65 or MS65+, but MS60.

An MS65 coin should have minimum marks and full luster; and no noticeable abrasion should be evident on Allen's cheek.

An MS65+ specimen, which will prove difficult to find, will be virtually flawless. It should not exhibit any friction on Allen's cheek. At the present time a superb coin can sometimes be purchased for a small premium of 15% to 20%. This premium may prove to be a bargain in future years.

On some uncirculated coins Ira Allen's lower hair curl appears to be a pronounced white color. This characteristic should not be confused with actual wear on a coin which has circulated.

Buying Tips

When purchasing a mint state Vermont Half Dollar inspect Allen's hair curl and cheek and the catamount's shoulder for signs of wear.

Make sure an MS65 specimen has full luster, minimum marks, and no noticeable abrasion or slide marks.

An MS65+ coin should have full, frosty mint bloom. In addition, it should not display any detracting marks, slide marks, or friction on Allen's face.

Booker T. Washington Memorial
Half Dollar

Net Mintage
(Note: The D&S mint marks can be found on the reverse under the log cabin.)

1946 :	1,000,546	1948 :	8,005	1950 :	6,004
1946D:	200,113	1948D:	8,005	1950D:	6,004
1946S:	500,279	1948S:	8,005	1950S:	512,091
1947 :	100,017	1949 :	6,004	1951 :	510,082
1947D:	100,017	1949D:	6,004	1951D:	7,004
1947S:	100,017	1949S:	6,004	1951S:	7,004

MS65 Retail Price Analysis

	1946PDS	1947PDS	1948PDS	
1970:	$11.00	$15.00	$21.00	
1979:	19.50	47.50	95.00	
Appreciation:	77%	217%	352%	

	1949PDS	1950PDS	1951PDS	Type
1970:	$ 34.00	$ 30.00	$30.00	$ 3.50
1979:	145.00	130.00	95.00	6.00
Appreciation:	326%	333%	217%	71%

Mint State Frequency (Type Coin Only)
- MS60 : 85%
- MS65 : 10%
- MS65+: 5%

Typical Mint State Specimen (Type Coin Only)
MS60: Numerous bag marks, excessive abrasion.

Comments

The Booker T. Washington Half Dollar, in relation to the tens of thousands of coins which remain in mint state condition, is a very difficult coin to find in Gem MS65 condition. It is extremely difficult to locate in true Superb MS65+ condition.

Although most mint state specimens grade MS60, because over three million coins were issued, thousands still will grade MS65. Bag quantities exist in uncirculated condition. Therefore, supply will probably exceed demand in the immediate future.

The market for these coins is sometimes subject to promotion by dealers and, as a result, a false market can be easily established. For example, one or two major dealers can promote this coin on the teletype circuits and raise wholesale bid and ask levels, while at the same time, unknown to collectors, other dealers are dumping their coins onto the market at prices 10% to 20% under bid! Do not be caught in this squeeze.

Many of this issue have been circulated. Many more remain in mint state condition and are marred by excessive abrasion on Washington's face; numerous bag marks also make this coin quite unattractive. These problems particularly plague the obverse of the coin, while the reverse usually is not as badly bruised. Uncirculated specimens with these problems should be graded MS60.

An MS65 piece should exhibit only minor abrasion and the bag marks should be at a minimum. It is possible to search through five or ten rolls and only find two or three gem pieces. However, because of limited demand for these coins only a small markup of about 10% to 20% should be paid for these specimens.

An MS65+ specimen, with full mint bloom and no detracting marks or abrasion, will prove to be very difficult to find. When located, however, one can usually be purchased for a premium of 20% to 25%.

The PDS sets of 1946 and 1947 are very plentiful and are not recommended for investment. The sets of 1948, 1949, 1950, and 1951, each with a set mintage of 8,005 or less, are relatively scarce. However, with a little persuasion on the collector's part, these sets, if really choice, can sometimes be purchased around the dealer's wholesale ask level.

Buying Tips

When purchasing a mint state Booker T. Washington Half Dollar inspect the cheekbone and the letters "FROM SLAVE CABIN TO HALL OF FAME" for signs of wear.

An MS65 specimen should exhibit full luster, minimum abrasion, and a few bag marks.

The search for a true Superb MS65+ coin, with full mint bloom and no detracting marks or abrasion, will be a very frustrating task for the collector.

When buying a PDS set examine each coin exactly as you would a type coin. If one or more of the three coins does not meet the standards for a gem coin do not purchase the set at MS65 prices. A PDS set's demand and price are lowered a great deal by the condition of the worst coin.

Washington-Carver
Half Dollar

Net Mintage
(Note: The D&S mint marks can be found on the reverse under the map of the U.S.)

1951 :	110,018	1952 :	2,006,292	1953 :	8,003	1954 :	12,006
1951D:	10,004	1952D:	8,006	1953D:	8,003	1954D:	12,006
1951S:	10,004	1952S:	8,006	1953S:	108,020	1954S:	122,024

MS65 Retail Price Analysis

	1951PDS	1952PDS	1953PDS	1954PDS	Type
1970:	$11.00	$18.00	$ 20.00	$11.00	$ 3.50
1979:	57.50	79.00	130.00	57.50	5.75
Appreciation:	423%	339%	550%	423%	64%

Mint State Frequency (Type Coin Only)
- MS60 : 90%
- MS65 : 9%
- MS65+: 1%

Typical Mint State Specimen (Type Coin Only)
MS60: Poorly struck, heavy gouges, excessive bag marks.

Comments

The Washington-Carver Half Dollar, in relation to the great numbers of specimens which remain in mint state condition, is a very difficult coin to find in Gem MS65 condition. It is almost impossible to locate in true Superb MS65+ condition.

Despite the fact most uncirculated pieces grade MS60, because over two million coins were minted, thousands of coins will still grade MS65. Like the B.T.W. Half Dollars, bag quantities exist in uncirculated condition. Therefore, the same investment comments which were made for the B.T.W. issues will generally hold true for the Washington-Carver coins.

Thousands of these coins have circulated. Many more remain in mint state condition, but most of these suffer from heavy gouges and bag marks and poor strikes. Uncirculated coins with these problems should be graded MS60.

An MS65 specimen should have full luster, a better than average strike, minimum bag marks, and no gouges. While readily available by the original roll, it is probable that only one or two pieces in each roll will grade MS65. However, because of limited demand for these coins only a small premium of about 10% to 20% (about $1.00) should be paid for a gem specimen.

An MS65+ piece, with full mint bloom, a sharp strike, and no gouges, slide marks, or detracting marks, will be extremely difficult to find. But when one is found it can usually be purchased for a premium of 20% to 25%.

All four PDS sets have relatively low set mintages. Despite this, an MS65 set can sometimes be purchased around the dealer's wholesale ask level.

Buying Tips

When purchasing a mint state Washington-Carver Half Dollar inspect the cheekbone and the letters "U.S.A." for signs of wear.

An MS65 specimen should be sharply struck and have full luster and minimum bag marks. In addition, it should not have any slide marks or gouges.

The search for a true MS65+ coin may be a frustrating task for the quality conscious collector.

When buying a PDS set examine each coin exactly as you would a type coin. If one or more of the three coins does not meet the standards for a gem coin do not purchase the set at MS65 prices. A PDS set's demand and price are lowered greatly by the condition of the worst coin.

Wisconsin Territorial Centennial
Half Dollar

Net Mintage
25,015

Mint State Frequency
MS60 : 35%
MS65 : 45%
MS65+: 20%

MS65 Retail Price Analysis
1970: $ 37.50
1979: 125.00
Appreciation: 233%

Typical Mint State Specimen
MS65: Full luster, minimum marks, no abrasion.

Comments

The 1936 Wisconsin Half Dollar, despite a relatively low mintage, is not a difficult coin to find in Gem MS65 or Superb MS65+ condition at the present.

Most Wisconsins remain in mint state condition. Some, however, exhibit abrasion on the hand and the badger and others display excessive handling marks. Uncirculated coins with these problems should be graded MS60. Because this issue is so readily available in MS65 or MS65+ condition today the purchase of MS60 pieces is not recommended for investment. For only a small premium of 10% to 15% a gem or superb piece usually can be purchased.

An MS65 coin should exhibit full luster, minimum marks, and no abrasion.

An MS65+ specimen will be virtually flawless and is one of the easiest lower mintage commemoratives to find in this condition. If purchased now for a modest premium, the collector will be making a sound decision because in the future top quality specimens will be in the greatest demand.

Buying Tips

When purchasing a mint state Wisconsin Half Dollar inspect the hand and the badger's shoulder for signs of wear.

Make certain an MS65 specimen has minimum marks, full mint bloom and no abrasion on the hand or badger.

An MS65+ piece should be virtually flawless and exhibit full, frosty luster.

Beware of the few cleaned coins which are unscrupulously offered as BU; they are easy to spot by the numerous hairlines, wear, and overall polished, chrome-like look.

York County, Maine Tercentenary
Half Dollar

Net Mintage
25,015

Mint State Frequency
MS60 : 35%
MS65 : 50%
MS65+: 15%

MS65 Retail Price Analysis
1970: $ 29.00
1979: 104.00
Appreciation: 328%

Typical Mint State Specimen
MS65: Full luster, minimum bag marks.

Comments

The 1936 York Half Dollar, despite its relatively low mintage, is not a difficult coin to find in Gem MS65 or Superb MS65+ condition.

Most Yorks remain in mint state condition today. However, some will exhibit numerous scattered bag marks, particularly on the cross on the shield on the obverse. Uncirculated coins with these marks should not be graded MS65 or MS65+, but MS60.

Like the Wisconsin, because this issue is so readily available in gem or superb condition today, purchase of MS60 pieces is not recommended for investment. For only a small premium of 10% to 15% an MS65 or MS65+ specimen can be obtained.

An MS65 specimen should have minimum bag marks and full luster.

An MS65+ piece will be virtually flawless and exhibit the most minute detail on the stockade on the reverse. Purchase of these quality coins is recommended because in the future they will be in the greatest demand by collectors.

Buying Tips

When purchasing a mint state York Half Dollar inspect the middle of the seal and the stockade for signs of wear.

Make certain an MS65 or MS65+ specimen exhibits full mint bloom and minimum marks. Also a superb specimen should display full detail on the stockade's tiny features, such as the door hinges.

Be on the lookout for the few cleaned pieces which are sometimes offered as BU; these can be differentiated from mint state specimens by the lack of natural luster and loss of detail on the reverse. In addition, cleaned coins will exhibit numerous hairlines.

CHAPTER IX
GOLD COMMEMORATIVES

Well, you've read the silver commemorative section of this book. How difficult can grading the gold commemoratives possibly be? After all, how many problems can these little golden beauties possibly display on their tiny surfaces? Do not be misled! Just because the gold pieces all look new, bright, and shiny does not mean they are all Unc!

The collecting of a complete gem or superb eleven piece gold commemorative set (disregarding the two Panama-Pacific $50 gold pieces) will be a very challenging task for many reasons.

1. Most of the mintages are very small.

2. Many of the issues were widely distributed to the public and, as a result, few hoards exist.

3. Many of the gold pieces were treated like souvenirs by their owners. The resultant improper preservation of these coins has decreased the already low potential collectible supply.

4. Because these eleven gold issues are much smaller than the silver issues it is often very difficult to detect problems like tiny nicks, scratches, abrasion, hairlines, and wear which so often appear on the fields and devices. While an experienced commemorative collector will often purchase the larger silver commemoratives without using a magnifying glass, most purchasers of the gold pieces will use one to look for the tiny, yet important, imperfections on these small coins. For example, the "typical" bag mark found on a Lafayette Dollar would be considered a terrible gash on a $1 gold commemorative. And the typical abrasion so often found on the gold $1 issues would be barely noticeable (and probably tolerated) on the larger silver coins. However, the small size of the $1 gold piece makes the abrasion relevant and, therefore, detracting to the connoisseur. In conclusion, small, yet detracting marks in the prominent locations on tiny coins should downgrade a gold commemorative coin from the MS65 or MS65+ grade to the MS60 grade.

The author has seen very few gem or superb eleven piece complete sets. There is usually at least one slider in most sets. To make matters worse, the slider is usually one of the key coins, e.g. the Lewis and Clark, Grant, or the $2½ Panama-Pacific. Before purchasing any complete set, the collector should very carefully examine each and every coin. Mistakes can be very expensive: a "gem" set containing an XF/AU Lewis and Clark, Grant, and $2½ Panama-Pacific is worth about $3,000 less than advertised! It is suggested the collector put together the gold (and the silver) set piece by piece and not search for the very elusive complete set.

CHAPTER X
INVESTMENT POTENTIAL OF GOLD COMMEMORATIVES

MS65 Retail Prices — Complete 11 Piece Set
1970:	$1,902.50
1971:	1,964.00
1972:	2,372.50
1973:	3,763.50
1974:	5,045.00
1975:	9,533.50
1976:	7,187.50
1977:	8,030.00
1978:	7,153.00
1979:	9,975.00

Since 1970, the gold issues have proven to be a fine investment (424% appreciation). However, since 1975, except for some speculative price fluctuations, the eleven piece set has experienced very little price appreciation. It is this author's belief that the gold commemoratives are also on the verge of a bull market. These coins are much scarcer in gem or superb condition than is generally believed. Assembling the complete set piece by piece in premium quality mint state condition will provide the collector or investor with almost as great a challenge as the fifty piece silver commemorative type set.

One major note of caution must be expressed at this point. There are not as many gold coin collectors as silver collectors. In fact, the gold commemorative market is less sophisticated than the silver commemorative market. Therefore, it may take a year or two longer for this series to "catch fire" like their silver cousins inevitably will. And when they do, price rises should prove to be very impressive.

Since most serious commemorative collectors insist on premium quality coins, MS60 specimens will probably appreciate at only a fraction of the percentage of the MS65 and MS65+ pieces. Therefore, grade each coin very carefully and insist on quality, and not quantity, to derive the maximum potential from your purchases.

CHAPTER XI
U.S. GOLD COMMEMORATIVES: A TYPE-BY-TYPE ANALYSIS

The following pages contain type-by-type analyses of the thirteen gold commemorative issues. The identical page format used for the silver issues has also been used for the gold commemoratives. (Refer to Chapter VIII for explanation of the analysis format.)

Grant Memorial
Gold Dollar

Net Mintage

Plain Variety:	5,000
Star Variety:	5,016

Mint State Frequency

MS60 :	55%
MS65 :	30%
MS65+:	15%

MS65 Retail Price Analysis

	Plain	Star
1970:	$ 250.00	$ 240.00
1979:	1,200.00	1,200.00
Appreciation:	380%	400%

Typical Mint State Specimen
MS60: Facial abrasion, detracting marks, poor luster.

Comments

The 1922 Grant Memorial Gold Dollar (both varieties) is one of the keys in the commemorative gold series. Few of these coins circulated. However, the majority of mint state specimens will not grade MS65 or MS65 +, but MS60 because of facial abrasion, detracting marks, and dull luster.

The purchase of MS60 pieces is not recommended for investment because they are unattractive and resale opportunities are limited. At present, an MS65 specimen sells for about 35% more than an MS60 piece. Since a gem Grant or Grant with Star is about two to three times scarcer than an average Unc specimen the premium appears to be very reasonable. In the future this markup should increase.

The Grant and the Grant with Star are about equal in rarity in MS65 or MS65+ condition.

Buying Tips

When purchasing a mint state Grant Gold Dollar inspect Grant's cheekbone and the leaves on the tree for signs of wear.

An MS65 specimen should exhibit nice luster. In addition, it should not display any detracting marks or facial abrasion.

An MS65+ piece will be very difficult to find, yet a premium of only 15% to 20% is presently charged. Purchase of virtually flawless superb specimens is strongly recommended at present prices.

One final note: BEWARE OF COUNTERFEITS! The Grant gold dollars are the most counterfeited of all the gold commemoratives. Every Grant gold dollar should be authenticated by a reliable authority.

Lewis & Clark Exposition
Gold Dollar

Net Mintage

    1904:   10,025
    1905:   10,041

Mint State Frequency
    MS60 :   75%
    MS65 :   20%
    MS65+:   5%

MS65 Retail Price Analysis

	1904	1905
1970:	$ 290.00	$ 300.00
1979:	1,450.00	1,450.00
Appreciation:	400%	383%

Typical Mint State Specimen
    MS60: Facial abrasion, detracting marks, poor luster.

Comments

The 1904 and 1905 Lewis & Clark Exposition Gold Dollars provide another excellent lesson for "mintage buffs" who believe mintage is the sole determination of rarity. For example, twice as many Lewis & Clark gold dollars were minted as the Grant gold dollars, yet the Lewis & Clark coins are much scarcer in mint state condition than the Grants. Most of the coins were sold to the non-collecting public who attended the Lewis & Clark Exposition in 1905. Very few found their way into collectors' hands. As a result, most specimens encountered today were not properly preserved. In mint state condition these two dates are very scarce but in circulated condition they are quite plentiful.

Most mint state specimens will grade MS60 because of detracting marks, facial abrasion, and poor luster. Because most knowledgeable commemorative collectors and investors demand gem and superb specimens for their collections the purchase of average Unc coins is not recommended for investment.

An MS65 or MS65 + Lewis & Clark specimen should sell for at least double the price of a typical MS60 specimen. However, do not expect to find one without considerable effort. They are extremely scarce in premium quality condition.

Both dates exist in prooflike condition. A gem prooflike should sell for a substantial premium over a normal luster coin. A very small quantity, perhaps 10 or 20, exist in true proof condition. Proofs are rare and are easily worth $4,000 + . However, make sure the coin is a proof and not a superb prooflike because the difference between the two is about $2,000!

Buying Tips

When purchasing a mint state Lewis & Clark Gold Dollar inspect the temples of Lewis & Clark for signs of wear.

An MS65 specimen should have full mint bloom and be free of abrasion and detracting marks.

An MS65+ piece should be virtually flawless.

It is strongly suggested that before purchasing a coin labeled as proof, the collector have it authenticated by a reliable authority.

Louisiana Purchase Exposition
Gold Dollar

Net Mintage

Jefferson:	17,000
McKinley:	17,500

Mint State Frequency

MS60 :	55%
MS65 :	30%
MS65+:	15%

MS65 Retail Price Analysis

	Jefferson	McKinley
1970:	$ 75.00	$ 70.00
1979:	465.00	465.00
Appreciation:	520%	564%

Typical Mint State Specimen
MS60: Softly struck, detracting marks, facial abrasion, dull luster.

Comments

The 1903 Louisiana Purchase Exposition Gold Dollars (Jefferson and McKinley) were the first commemorative gold coins struck. Because many of these coins were sold to the general public, they suffered from abuse (e.g. cleaning, carrying as pocket pieces, improper storage).

The majority of uncirculated specimens will grade MS60 because of poor luster, a soft srike, facial abrasion, and detracting marks. Average Unc specimens are not too attractive and are not recommended for investment.

An MS65 specimen presently sells for about 30% more than an MS60 piece. This price spread will undoubtedly widen in the future when collector and investor demand for gem commemorative gold coins increases.

An MS65+ piece, with full, blazing mint bloom and no noticeable impairments, is beautiful and can sometimes be purchased for an additional markup of 15% to 20%. The purchase of truly superb gems is recommended for long term investment.

Both varieties exist in prooflike condition. In addition 50 (or 100, depending on which record one believes) proofs of each type were made. A gem prooflike Jefferson or McKinley is extremely scarce and will often sell for double the price of a normal luster MS65 or MS65+ coin. True proofs are rare and have recently sold in the $2,500 range. Make sure a coin labeled proof is authenticated because the difference between a superb prooflike and a proof is about $1,500!

Buying Tips

When purchasing a mint state Louisiana Purchase/Jefferson or McKinley Gold Dollar inspect Jefferson's or McKinley's cheekbone on the obverse and the lettering on the reverse for signs of wear.

An MS65 specimen should be free of detracting marks and facial abrasion. In addition, it should be sharply struck and have full mint bloom.

An MS65+ piece should be virtually flawless and will prove very difficult to find.

Make sure a coin offered as a proof is authenticated. A proof will exhibit much greater detail, particularly in the hair of Jefferson or McKinley, than a business strike.

McKinley Memorial
Gold Dollar

Net Mintage

1916:	9,977
1917:	10,000

Mint State Frequency

MS60 :	60%
MS65 :	20%
MS65+:	20%

MS65 Retail Price Analysis

	1916	1917
1970:	$ 70.00	$140.00
1979:	480.00	520.00
Appreciation:	586%	271%

Typical Mint State Specimen
MS60: Poorly struck, dull luster, facial abrasion, detracting marks.

Comments
The 1916 and 1917 McKinley Memorial Gold Dollars are becoming increasingly difficult to acquire in premium quality mint state condition. Even though most McKinleys remain in mint state condition the majority will only grade MS60 because of numerous problems: poor luster, a weak strike, facial abrasion, and detracting marks. The purchase of MS60 pieces is not recommended for investment because their resaleability is not good.

An MS65 specimen only costs about 20% to 25% more than an MS60 piece. This is a small premium to pay to virtually guarantee the coin's resaleability in the future.

An MS65+ piece should be virtually flawless and can sometimes be purchased for a surprisingly modest markup of 15% to 20%. Expect this premium to increase in the future.

Despite the mintages being about equal, the 1917 issue is a bit scarcer than the 1916. In the past it sold for about double the 1916's price. Today it commands a more reasonable premium of 10% to 15%.

Buying Tips
When purchasing a mint state McKinley Gold Dollar inspect McKinley's temple and the middle and top of the Memorial for signs of wear.

An MS65 specimen should exhibit full mint bloom and a nice strike. In addition, it should not display any facial abrasion or detracting marks.

On occasion, either date can be found prooflike for a 15% to 25% premium. The purchase of prooflikes is recommended for long term investment.

Panama-Pacific Exposition
Gold Dollar

Net Mintage
15,000

Mint State Frequency
MS60 :   45%
MS65 :   40%
MS65+:   15%

MS65 Retail Price Analysis
1970: $ 65.00
1979:   610.00
Appreciation: 838%

Typical Mint State Specimen
MS60: Dull luster, facial abrasion, detracting marks.

Comments

The 1915-S Panama-Pacific Exposition Gold Dollar is probably the easiest commemorative gold dollar to find in gem MS65 or Superb MS65+ condition.

However, some have circulated and many have been abused and exhibit dull luster, excessive marks, and facial abrasion. Mint state pieces with these problems should not be graded MS65 or MS65+, but MS60. Average Unc pieces are not recommended for investment.

An MS65 coin should have full mint bloom and should not exhibit any facial abrasion or detracting marks.

An MS65+ specimen can sometimes be purchased for a rather modest 15% to 25% premium. In this condition the coins are very attractive and should prove to be an excellent long term investment.

Buying Tips

When purchasing a mint state Panama-Pacific Exposition Gold Dollar inspect the laborer's cheek and cap brim and the words ONE DOLLAR for signs of wear.

Mint state specimens which exhibit poor luster, facial abrasion, detracting marks, and a weak strike should be graded MS60.

An MS65 or MS65+ piece should be free of noticeable impairments and possess a full mint bloom.

Counterfeits of this issue, as well as all issues of Commemorative Gold, exist. Make sure you buy your coins from a reliable and knowledgeable source.

Panama-Pacific Exposition
Quarter Eagle

Net Mintage
6,749

Mint State Frequency
MS60 : 80%
MS65 : 15%
MS65+ : 5%

MS65 Retail Price Analysis
1970: 330.00
1979: 1,850.00
Appreciation: 461%

Typical Mint State Specimen
MS60: Softly struck, dull luster, excessive marks, abrasion.

Comments
The 1915-S Panama-Pacific Quarter Eagle ($2½) is the rarest commemorative gold coin to find in mint state condition in the eleven piece set.

Most specimens have circulated or been abused. The great majority of the few hundred surviving mint state specimens will only grade MS60 because of numerous problems: abrasion, a soft strike, excessive marks, and dull luster. Average Unc specimens, which sell for 60% to 70% of MS65 pieces, are not very attractive and are not recommended for investment.

An MS65 Panama-Pacific $2½ should be sharply struck and exhibit full luster. In addition, it should be free of abrasion and detracting marks. Very few gem Panama-Pacifics survive today.

An MS65+ specimen should be at least 90% fully struck and virtually flawless. A superb gem is extremely scarce but occasionally can be found for a 15% to 25% premium. Purchase of superb specimens is recommended for excellent long term price appreciation.

A collector trying to assemble a Superb MS65+ Pan-Pac "mini-set", consisting of the half dollar and the gold dollar and quarter eagle, will find this task extremely difficult, yet very rewarding when it is accomplished!

Buying Tips
When purchasing a mint state Panama-Pacific Quarter Eagle inspect Columbia's knee and the eagle's left leg (near the breast) for signs of wear. Because most Pan-Pacs were softly struck, be certain not to confuse a weak strike for wear. A circulated specimen will exhibit a luster "break" and tiny, crisscrossing, friction lines at the point of wear.

An MS65 or MS65+ specimen should be sharply struck and have full mint bloom. In addition, be sure the piece does not exhibit abrasion or any detracting marks.

Beware of counterfeits.

Panama-Pacific Exposition
Fifty Dollar Gold (Round)

Net Mintage
483

Mint State Frequency
MS60 : 15%
MS65 : 65%
MS65+: 20%

MS65 Retail Price Analysis
1970: 5,750
1979: 16,500
Appreciation: 187%

Typical Mint State Specimen
MS65: Full Mint bloom, some marks, usually well hidden by the design; no abrasions.

Comments
The Panama-Pacific Round Fifty Dollar piece, while not being especially rare, is much more difficult to locate as an individual item than is the Octagonal, as most of the pieces are included in complete sets. Of the entire mintage, the survival rate is probably over 75%. Its value is sustained by a tremendous demand attributed to its uniqueness as the only (including its Octagonal counterpart) Fifty Dollar coin issued by the United States Mint, and to its tremendous beauty.

Generally speaking, superb pieces, when located, can be purchased at relatively small premiums over average examples.

Buying Tips
The high points are on Minerva's cheekbone, and the top tip of the Owl's left wing. These areas should be checked for wear or abrasion. Because of the heavy weight of the coin, and the softness of the gold, the coins were subject to some large marks. Oftentimes, these marks are well hidden by the design of the coin. Because of the frequency with which the marks are encountered, one should not become overly concerned about one or two marks. These marks should be considered, however.

Panama-Pacific Exposition
Fifty Dollar Gold (Octagonal)

Net Mintage
645

Mint State Frequency
MS60 : 25%
MS65 : 60%
MS65+ : 15%

MS65 Retail Price Analysis
1970: 4,500
1979: 13,500
Appreciation: 200%

Typical Mint State Specimen
MS65: Full Mint bloom, some marks, usually well hidden by the design; no abrasions.

Comments
The Panama-Pacific Exposition Octagonal Fifty Dollar piece, for an expensive coin, is a very easy coin to locate. The survival rate of the entire mintage is probably over 70%. Its value is sustained by a tremendous demand attributed to its uniqueness as the only (including its Round counterpart) Fifty Dollar coin issued by the United States Mint, and to its tremendous beauty.

The Octagonal issue has a larger incidence of problems than does the Round, primarily because more Octagonals were sold individually, outside of the complete set. Consequently, they were more often improperly housed and cared for.

Generally speaking, superb pieces, when located, may be purchased at relatively small premiums over average examples.

Buying Tips
The high points are on Minerva's cheekbone, and the top tip of the Owl's left wing. These areas should be checked for wear or abrasion. Because of the heavy weight of the coin, and the softness of the gold, the coins were subject to some large marks. Oftentimes, these marks are well hidden by the design of the coin. Because of the frequency with which the marks are encountered, one should not become overly concerned about one or two marks. These marks should be considered, however.

Sesquicentennial of American Independence
Quarter Eagle

Net Mintage
46,019

Mint State Frequency
MS60 : 50%
MS65 : 35%
MS65+ : 15%

MS65 Retail Price Analysis
1970: $ 72.50
1979: 285.00
Appreciation: 293%

Typical Mint State Specimen
MS60: Weakly struck, abrasion, excessive marks.

Comments
The Sesquicentennial Quarter Eagle ($2½) is the most plentiful of all the gold commemorative issues. In comparison, it is quite common in mint state condition. Like its half dollar counterpart, many pieces circulated and will grade XF/AU.

A great number of uncirculated pieces were not properly preserved and will grade MS60 because of abrasion and detracting marks. In addition, many coins were poorly struck. Mint state pieces exhibiting these problems should not be graded MS65 or MS65+, but MS60. Average Unc specimens are not recommended for investment.

An MS65 specimen should be sharply struck and not exhibit any detracting marks or abrasion. For a modest premium of 10% to 20% a gem piece can be purchased.

An MS65+ coin should be virtually flawless and can be purchased for a small markup of 15% to 25%. Superb pieces are underrated and should show the greatest percentage price appreciation in the future.

Buying Tips
When purchasing a mint state Sesquicentennial Quarter Eagle inspect the bottom of the scroll and the Independence Hall tower for signs of wear.

Be certain an MS65 or MS65+ specimen is sharply struck and exhibits full mint bloom. Also it should not display any abrasion or detracting marks.

On the reverse of all gold Sesquis seen by the author is a die defect located in the upper left field at nine and ten o'clock. This defect should not affect the condition of the coin.

CHAPTER XII
1979: THE YEAR OF THE COMMEMORATIVE?

Some interesting trends in the commemorative coin market are rapidly developing as 1979 begins. The wholesale market is stirring and prices are escalating to record levels. Superb quality (MS65+) specimens are bringing record prices at auction. For example:

Type	Price Realized	Auction House
Bay Bridge	$ 240	Paramount
Cleveland	95	Paramount
Connecticut	230	Ivy
Hudson	1,050	Paramount
Lexington-Concord	103	Ivy
Lincoln-Illinois	140	Ivy
Long Island	96	Ivy
Monroe	290	Paramount
Roanoke	180	Ivy
San Diego (1936-D)	350	Paramount
Spanish Trail	850	Bowers & Ruddy

At three major coin conventions, this author witnessed the following transactions:

Isabella (MS65+)	$ 750
Columbian (MS65+)	200
Missouri (MS65)	1,900 (!)
Monroe (MS65+)	150 (wholesale!)
1933-D Oregon Trail (MS65+)	315

The quality craze, which is so prevalent in other coin series, appears to have finally arrived with commemoratives! Truly exceptional pieces are selling for substantial premiums to both dealers and collectors. The days of purchasing the scarce gem and superb specimens at wholesale ask or slightly above are over.

ONE WORD OF CAUTION. Some unscrupulous dealers who constantly overgrade their coins are changing their tactics. In the past, they would offer their "super-slider gems" at 50% to 60% of the true market price. Now they are offering many of these same pieces at double the market price! The psychology involved is rather shrewd. Many collectors have been warned that superb coins cost substantially more than the average specimens. So, the "cleaning merchant" reasons, let them pay superb prices if that's what they want!

Remember, a high price for a coin is NO GUARANTEE OF HIGH QUALITY. For example, at a recent New York coin convention this author scrutinized one dealer's commemorative offerings and the findings were startling:

	Dealer's Grade	Price	Actual Grade	Actual Worth
Columbian	"Gem Proof"	$ 700	Cleaned Proof-Like	$ 10
Panama-Pacific	"MS65+"	2,100	Toned AU	$125
Lafayette	"Gem Toned Unc"	4,000	Toned AU	$250
Total		$6,800		$385

Anyone purchasing these specimens at the alleged grade and stated prices would have lost a small fortune. Collector: Educate Thyself! It will not be easy and it will take time but the rewards, both aesthetic and financial, can be fantastic. Conversely, if the collector chooses to spend only a little time in learning all the nuances of grading and investing in commemorative coins, the results could prove to be disastrous.

Like most things in life, the rewards usually are obtained by those people who enjoy what they are doing and work the hardest at it. These people can generally be seen driving Cadillacs or some other fancy car. Those who choose to take the easy way out and "just get by" usually reap their just rewards also. Such people can often be seen driving the Edsels of this world. Which car do you choose to drive?

CHAPTER XIII
STATISTICAL TABLE FOR U.S. SILVER COMMEMORATIVES

The statistical table for silver commemoratives (and for the gold commemoratives, Chapter XIV) includes 10 year price projections for MS65 specimens. These price projections are merely the author's opinion of what the future might hold for the commemorative investor. The projections are based on three assumptions:
1. Commemoratives are very undervalued in relation to many other coin issues.
2. Inflation will continue at its current horrendous pace. (In effect, today's dollar will be worth about 50 cents in 1989.)
3. Investors wil continue to flee from traditional low yielding investments (e.g. stocks, bonds, savings accounts) and search for lucrative and proven alternative investment sources. As a result, the demand for quality rare coins should constantly increase while the available supply of gem and superb pieces simultaneously dwindles.

The author makes no claim to being a professional soothsayer. Therefore, no guarantees can be made that any of these prices will come true. However, it will be interesting to see how close (or how far off) they are in 1989. One of the niceties of ten year forecasting is that few people will remember if the projected prices do not materialize. However, be assured that if they are "on the money" no one will be allowed to forget.

	Net Mintage	MS65 Retail Price 1970	1979	1989 Projection
Isabella	24,124	82.50	625.00	2,500.00
Lafayette	36,026	195.00	3,750.00	12,500.00
Alabama 2x2	6,006	72.50	600.00	2,750.00
Alabama	59,038	52.50	465.00	2,500.00
Albany	17,671	55.00	185.00	450.00
Antietam	18,028	82.50	250.00	525.00
'35 Arkansas-PDS	—	40.00	195.00	775.00
'36 Arkansas-PDS	—	40.00	160.00	650.00
'37 Arkansas-PDS	—	42.50	205.00	815.00
'38 Arkansas-PDS	—	70.00	475.00	2,650.00
'39 Arkansas-PDS	—	325.00	1,300.00	4,500.00
Arkansas-Type Coin	—	14.00	55.00	140.00
Bay Bridge	71,424	25.00	66.00	155.00
'34 Boone	10,007	20.00	85.00	535.00
'35 Boone-PDS	—	48.00	195.00	775.00
'35/34 Boone-PDS	—	300.00	1,260.00	3,900.00
'36 Boone-PDS	—	48.00	168.00	700.00
'37 Boone-PDS	—	175.00	470.00	2,500.00

	Net Mintage	MS65 Retail Price 1970	1979	1989 Projection
'38 Boone-PDS	—	290.00	1,075.00	3,600.00
Boone-Type Coin	—	15.00	58.00	135.00
Bridgeport	25,015	30.00	103.00	280.00
California	86,594	26.00	107.50	375.00
Cincinnati-PDS	—	405.00	1,050.00	2,750.00
Cincinnati-Type Coin	—	135.00	330.00	885.00
Cleveland	50,030	18.50	42.50	90.00
Columbia-PDS	—	165.00	655.00	1,500.00
Columbia-Type Coin	—	55.00	205.00	475.00
'92 Columbian	950,000	7.00	42.50	375.00
'93 Columbian	1,550,405	5.50	42.50	375.00
Connecticut	25,018	50.00	185.00	450.00
Delaware	20,993	48.00	145.00	525.00
Elgin	20,015	41.00	122.00	350.00
Gettysburg	26,928	44.00	195.00	620.00
Grant	67,405	26.00	106.00	575.00
Grant with Star	4,256	125.00	1,050.00	7,750.00
Hawaiian	9,958	485.00	1,775.00	6,250.00
Hudson	10,008	250.00	595.00	1,750.00
Huguenot-Walloon	142,080	26.00	100.00	395.00
Iowa	100,057	24.00	51.00	80.00
Lexington-Concord	162,013	15.00	60.00	275.00
Lincoln-Illinois	100,058	26.00	82.00	350.00
Long Island	81,826	18.00	57.50	150.00
Lynchburg	20,013	38.00	124.00	465.00
Maine	50,028	25.00	115.00	550.00
Maryland	25,015	36.50	115.00	485.00
Missouri 2★4	5,000	155.00	990.00	4,500.00
Missouri	15,428	150.00	990.00	4,600.00
Monroe	274,077	18.00	91.00	400.00
New Rochelle	15,266	67.50	245.00	500.00
Norfolk	16,936	57.50	237.00	425.00
'26 Oregon Trail	47,955	15.00	85.00	225.00
'26-S Oregon Trail	83,055	15.00	85.00	225.00
'28 Oregon Trail	6,028	20.00	215.00	950.00
'33-D Oregon Trail	5,008	35.00	230.00	1,025.00
'34-D Oregon Trail	7,006	16.00	180.00	875.00
'36 Oregon Trail	10,006	15.00	92.00	600.00
'36-S Oregon Trail	5,006	20.00	205.00	1,000.00
'37-D Oregon Trail	12,008	15.00	90.00	525.00
'38 Oregon Trail-PDS	—	45.00	420.00	900.00
'39 Oregon Trail-PDS	—	125.00	555.00	2,000.00
Oregon Trail-Type Coin	—	15.00	85.00	225.00
Panama-Pacific	27,134	85.00	980.00	4,750.00
'20 Pilgrim	152,112	18.00	57.50	175.00

	Net Mintage	MS65 Retail Price 1970	MS65 Retail Price 1979	1989 Projection
'21 Pilgrim	20,053	66.00	126.50	510.00
Rhode Island-PDS	—	52.00	260.00	700.00
Rhode Island-Type Coin	—	17.50	85.00	225.00
Roanoke	29,030	28.00	99.00	285.00
Robinson-Arkansas	25,265	24.00	86.00	345.00
'35-S San Diego	70,132	17.00	55.00	240.00
'36-D San Diego	30,092	19.00	98.00	325.00
Sesquicentennial	141,120	17.50	57.00	175.00
Spanish Trail	10,008	235.00	525.00	1,650.00
Stone Mountain	1,314,709	12.00	33.50	70.00
'34 Texas	61,463	19.00	51.00	95.00
'35 Texas-PDS	—	50.00	175.00	500.00
'36 Texas-PDS	—	50.00	172.50	525.00
'37 Texas-PDS	—	55.00	235.00	800.00
'38 Texas-PDS	—	110.00	515.00	1,750.00
Texas-Type Coin	—	17.00	54.00	105.00
Ft. Vancouver	14,994	92.50	435.00	1,500.00
Vermont	28,142	38.00	137.50	600.00
'46 Booker T. Washington-PDS	—	11.00	19.50	45.00
'47 Booker T. Washington-PDS	—	15.00	47.50	100.00
'48 Booker T. Washington-PDS	—	21.00	95.00	325.00
'49 Booker T. Washington-PDS	—	34.00	145.00	500.00
'50 Booker T. Washington-PDS	—	30.00	130.00	475.00
'51 Booker T. Washington-PDS	—	30.00	95.00	425.00
Booker T. Washington-Type Coin	—	3.50	6.00	14.00
'51 Washington-Carver-PDS	—	11.00	57.50	250.00
'52 Washington-Carver-PDS	—	18.00	79.00	275.00
'53 Washington-Carver-PDS	—	20.00	130.00	325.00
'54 Washington-Carver-PDS	—	11.00	57.50	230.00
Washington-Carver-Type Coin	—	3.50	5.75	14.00
Wisconsin	25,015	37.50	125.00	400.00
York	25,015	29.00	104.00	425.00
50 Piece Type Set		2,927.00	14,602.75	51,668.00
144 Piece Type Set		5,922.50	28,343.50	107,065.00

CHAPTER XIV
STATISTICAL TABLE FOR U.S. GOLD COMMEMORATIVES

	Net Mintage	MS65 Retail Price 1970	MS65 Retail Price 1979	1989 Projection
Grant	5,000	$250.00	$1,200.00	$3,500.00
Grant with Star	5,016	240.00	1,200.00	3,500.00
'04 Lewis & Clark	10,025	290.00	1,450.00	4,500.00
'05 Lewis & Clark	10,041	300.00	1,450.00	4,500.00
Louisiana Purchase/Jefferson	17,500	75.00	465.00	1,325.00
Louisiana Purchase/McKinley	17,500	70.00	465.00	1,325.00
'16 McKinley	9,977	70.00	480.00	1,325.00
'17 McKinley	10,000	140.00	520.00	1,375.00
Panama-Pacific $1	15,000	65.00	610.00	1,150.00
Panama-Pacific $2½	6,749	330.00	1,850.00	5,500.00
Panama-Pacific $50 (Round)	483	5,750.00	16,500.00	49,500.00
Panama-Pacific $50 (Octagonal)	645	4,500.00	13,500.00	40,500.00
Sesquicentennial $2½	46,019	72.50	285.00	625.00
11 Piece Set (Excluding the $50 pieces)	—	1,902.50	9,975.00	28,625.00

CHAPTER XV
IMPORTANT GRADING HIGHLIGHTS FOR SILVER COMMEMORATIVES

The chart below details the major problems which generally are found on each Average Unc (MS60) type coin. An issue exhibiting a particular problem will have an asterisk (*) in the appropriate column. There are exceptions for every coin and in these cases experience in grading and dealing with a knowledgeable commemorative dealer are important.

Type	Noticeable Abrasion	Detracting Marks	Poor Strike	Poor Luster	Light Cleaning
Isabella	*			*	*
Lafayette	*	*	*	*	*
Alabama	*	*	*	*	*
Albany	*	*			
Antietam		*			
Arkansas	*	*	*	*	*
Bay Bridge	*	*			*
Boone		*			
Bridgeport	*	*			
California	*	*			*
Cincinnati	*	*	*		*
Cleveland		*			
Columbia, S.C.				*	
Columbian	*	*	*	*	*
Connecticut	*	*	*		
Delaware	*	*	*		*
Elgin		*	*		
Gettysburg		*			
Grant	*	*	*	*	*
Grant with Star	*	*	*	*	*
Hawaiian	*	*		*	*
Hudson	*	*	*	*	*
Huguenot-Walloon		*		*	
Iowa		*			
Lexington-Concord	*	*	*	*	*
Lincoln-Illinois	*	*			*
Long Island	*	*			*
Lynchburg	*	*			
Maine		*	*	*	*
Maryland	*	*	*		
Missouri	*			*	*
Monroe	*	*	*	*	*
New Rochelle	*	*			
Norfolk		*			*

Type	Noticeable Abrasion	Detracting Marks	Poor Strike	Poor Luster	Light Cleaning
Oregon Trail		*			
Panama-Pacific	*	*	*	*	*
Pilgrim		*	*		*
Rhode Island		*			
Roanoke		*			*
Robinson-Arkansas	*	*			
San Diego	*	*			
Sesquicentennial	*	*	*	*	*
Spanish Trail	*	*			*
Stone Mountain		*	*		*
Texas	*				
Ft. Vancouver	*	*	*		*
Vermont	*	*			
Booker T. Washington	*	*		*	
Washington-Carver		*	*	*	
Wisconsin	*	*			
York		*			

CHAPTER XVI
A CHRONOLOGY OF COMMEMORATIVE COINAGE

Date	Type	Designer
1892, 1893	Columbian Exposition	Barber, Morgan
1893	Isabella Quarter	Barber
1900	Lafayette Dollar	Barber
1915-S	Panama-Pacific Exposition	Barber
1918	Lincoln-Illinois Centennial	Morgan, Sinnock
1920	Maine Centennial	de Francisci
1920, 1921	Pilgrim Tercentenary	Dallin
1921	Alabama Centennial	L.G. Fraser
1921	Missouri Centennial	Aitken
1922	Grant Memorial	L.G. Fraser
1923-S	Monroe Doctrine Centennial	Beach
1924	Huguenot-Walloon Tercentenary	Morgan
1925-S	California Diamond Jubilee	Mora
1925	Lexington-Concord Sesquicentennial	Beach
1925	Stone Mountain Memorial	Borglum
1925	Fort Vancouver, Centennial	L.G. Fraser
1926	Sesquicentennial of American Independence	Sinnock
1926-1939	Oregon Trail Memorial	L.G. Fraser
1927	Vermont Sesquicentennial	Keck
1928	Hawaiian Sesquicentennial	J.M. Fraser, Beach
1934	Maryland Tercentenary	Schuler
1934-1938	Daniel Boone Bicentennial	Lukeman
1934-1938	Texas Independence Centennial	Coppini
1935	Connecticut Tercentenary	Kreiss
1935-1939	Arkansas Centennial	Burr, Kreiss
1935	Hudson, New York Sesquicentennial	Beach
1935-S, 1936-D	San Diego, California-Pacific Exposition	Aitken
1935	Old Spanish Trail	Hoffecker
1936	Albany, New York	Lathrop
1936-S	Bay Bridge (San Francisco-Oakland)	Schneir
1936	Bridgeport, Connecticut Centennial	Kneiss
1936	Cincinnati Musical Center	Ortmayer
1936	Cleveland, Great Lakes Exposition	Putnam
1936	Columbia, South Carolina Sesquicentennial	Davidson
1936	Delaware Tercentenary	Schmitz
1936	Elgin, Illinois Centennial	Rovelstad
1936	Battle of Gettysburg	Vittor
1936	Long Island Tercentenary	Weinman
1936	Lynchburg, Virginia Sesquicentennial	Keck
1936	Norfolk, Virginia Bicentennial	Simpson

Date	Type	Designer
1936	Rhode Island (Providence) Tercentenary	Carey, Benson
1936	Robinson-Arkansas Centennial	Burr
1936	Wisconsin Territorial Centennial	Parsons, Hawkins
1936	York County, Maine Centennial	Rich
1937	Battle of Antietam	Simpson
1937	Roanoke Island, North Carolina	Simpson
1938	New Rochelle, New York	Lathrop
1946	Iowa Centennial	Pietz
1946-1951	Booker T. Washington Memorial	Hathaway
1951-1954	Washington-Carver	Hathaway

Gold Commemoratives

Date	Type	Designer
1903	Louisiana Purchase Exposition Dollars	Barber
1904, 1905	Lewis and Clark Exposition Dollars	Barber
1915-S	Panama-Pacific Exposition Dollar	Keck
1915-S	Panama-Pacific Exposition Quarter Eagle	Barber
1915-S	Panama-Pacific Exposition $50 (Round)	Aitken
1915-S	Panama-Pacific Exposition $50 (Octagonal)	Aitken
1916, 1917	McKinley Memorial Dollar	Barber, Morgan
1922	Grant Memorial Dollars	L.G. Fraser
1926	Sesquicentennial of American Independence Quarter Eagle	Sinnock

CHAPTER XVII
RECOMMENDED READING

The author agrees with the saying in numismatic circles "Buy the book before you buy the coin". The following is a list of books, newspapers, and newsletters which all commemorative collectors should consider for their libraries.

Books
1. **An Illustrated History of U.S. Commemorative Coinage,** by Don Taxay.
   (Arco Publishing Company, Inc.)
   This book is a fascinating behind-the-scenes history of our commemorative coinage. It details from records of the Commission of Fine Arts the true story behind the creation of all the commemorative issues. In addition, numerous artists' proposed sketches and designs are included in this book.

2. **United States Commemorative Coinage,** by Arlie Slabaugh.
   (Western Publishing Company, Inc.)
   This book, to a great extent, describes the historical events which each coin issue commemorates. History "buffs" will enjoy reading this book.

2. **Counterfeit Mis-Struck and Unofficial U.S. Coins,** by Don Taxay.
   (Arco Publishing Company, Inc.)
   Another work by Taxay, it is an excellent guide for the general detection of struck and cast counterfeits, electrotypes, and altered coins. Of particular interest to commemorative collectors is the section dealing with the Grant with Star Half Dollar.

4. **A Guide Book of United State Coins,** by R.S. Yeoman.
   (Western Publishing Company, Inc.)
   The "Red Book", now in its 32nd printing, is the bible of coin collectors everywhere. It is a basic book for any collector and is a must in any numismatic library.

Newspapers
5. **Coin World** (Box 150, Sidney, Ohio 45365).
   A weekly newspaper, it has the largest distribution (about 100,000) of any coin newspaper in the country. A subscription will provide the collector with many enjoyable hours of reading per week.

6. **Numismatic News** (Krause Publications, 700 East State St., Iola, Wisconsin 54945).
   Another weekly coin newspaper, it is about one quarter the size of **Coin World.** Its Coin Market section provides the collector with a generally reliable weekly coin pricing guide.

Newsletters
7. **Coin Dealer Newsletter** (Box 2308, Hollywood, CA. 90028).
   This weekly publication, a must for the serious collector or investor, is the "Wall Street Journal" of the wholesale dealer-to-dealer coin market. The Bid/Ask quotes for commemoratives should be used as a general guide for the collector. These wholesale quotes are very reliable for the more common issues selling for about $125 and less. However, for the much scarcer issues, e.g. Lafayette, Isabella, Alabama, etc., a dealer will usually have to pay the "Ask" or more for properly graded specimens.

At the present time, there is only a small price spread between MS60 (Average Uncirculated) and MS65 (Gem BU) Bid/Ask levels for commemorative issues. In the future, the collector should expect this quality price spread to considerably widen as the demand for choice and gem specimens constantly increases.

8. **The Forecaster** (19623 Ventura Blvd., Tarzana CA. 91356).

Published 44 times a year, the prestigious **Forecaster** regularly provides insightful analysis of current and projected economic trends. Eight pages in length, it usually includes at least two pages of coin recommendations in each issue. Because of its large readership and excellent track record of spotting undervalued coins, a subscription to this publication might prove fruitful for the investor.

9. **The Rosen Numismatic Advisory** (P.O. Box 231, East Meadow, N.Y. 11554).

The "RNA" is a monthly publication which deals strictly with the coin market. The serious collector or investor will enjoy reading the many insights and recommendations about the various segments of the wholesale and retail rare coin market. Included in many issues are detailed investment analyses of different coin series and "behind-the-scenes" looks at the workings of the coin industry.

— NOTES —

— NOTES —

NOTES

— **NOTES** —